UNNATURAL

techno-theory for a contaminated culture

UNDERGROUND

UNNATURAL - techno-theory for a contaminated culture
Edited by Matthew Fuller

Design by If Graphics

First published 1994 by Underground
PO Box 3285, London, SW2 3NN, UK.

ISBN 1 899037 00 4

British Library Catalogue in Publication Data
A catalogue record for this book is available from the British Library

Cover photo, *Electronic Phallus captured by X-Ray in Moral Total Exclusion Zone* courtesy of Hilaire and Robin Rimbaud.

Printed by Total Central Limited, 4 Farnham Royal, Kennington Lane, London, SE11

Acknowledgements:

This book has taken about a year to stick together, so thanks are due to all those who've helped it on its way: all the contributors of course, but in particular, Mandie Beuzeval, Sadie Plant, Graham Harwood and Simon Pope deserve either a good kicking or the Order of Lenin. Thanks also to the Fast Breeder massive for making itself happen, AK and Counter Productions for making this type of publishing possible, and for general incitement; Steve Edgell, Jason Skeet, Stefan Szczelkun, Bruce, Calum Selkirk, Stewart Home, Cat and the House of Homocult.

If you'd like a copy of this book but can't afford the cover price, get in touch and we can sort something out.

CONTENTS

Perpetrators indicated by icon at corner of page

THIRD TERMINAL
Stephen Metcalf

BANDITO
Maxine Boobyer

THE SHAKE AND DECODER HISTORY & DECODER DICTIONARY
Decoder

ALL NEW GEN
VNS-Matrix

N© N© N© N© N© N© N© N© N© N© N© N© THERE'S N© LIMIT
Mark Pawson

LIES
Graham Harwood

TALES OF PAGEANT AND PANTOMIME
a technological narrative for a virtual aristocracy
Richard Wright

Sadie Plant
and
Nick Land

Chaos

CYBERPOSITIVE

Catastrophe is the past coming apart.

Anastrophe is the future coming together.

Seen from within history, divergence is reaching critical proportions. From the matrix, crisis is a convergence misinterpreted by mankind.

Chaos

The media are choked with stories about global warming and ozone depletion, HIV and AIDS, plagues of drugs and software viruses, nuclear proliferation, the planetary disintegration of economic management, breakdown of the family, waves of migrants and refugees, subsidence of the nation state into its terminal dementia, societies grated open by the underclass, urban cores in flames, suburbia under threat, fission, schizophrenia, loss of control.

No wonder the earth is said to be hurtling into catastrophe. Climate change, ecological and immunity collapse, ideological upheaval, war and earthquake: California is waiting for The Big One. This is an age of crack-ups and melt-downs.

Rotted by digital contagions, modernity is falling to bits. Lenin, Mussolini, and Roosevelt concluded modern humanism by exhausting the possibilities of economic planning. Runaway capitalism has broken through all the social control mechanisms, accessing inconceivable alienations. Capital clones itself with increasing disregard for heredity, becoming abstract positive feedback, organizing itself. Turbular finance drifts across the global network.

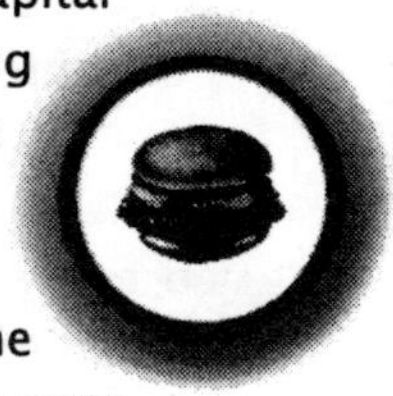

Wiener is one of the great modernists, defining cybernetics as the science of communication and control; a tool for human dominion over nature and history, a defence against the cyberpathology of markets. His propaganda against positive feedback - quantizing it as amplification within an invariable metric - has been highly influential, establishing a cybernetics of stability fortified against the future. There is no space in such a theory for anything truly cyberpositive, subtle or intelligent beyond the objectivity required for human comprehension. Nevertheless, beyond the event horizon of human science, even the investigation of self-stabilizing or cybernegative objects is inevitably enveloped by exploratory or cyberpositive processes.

The modern Human Security System might even have appeared with Wiener's subliminal insight that everything cyberpositive is an enemy of mankind. Evolving out of work on weaponry guidance systems, his was an attempt to enslave cybernetics to a general defence technology against alien invasion. Cybernetics was itself to be kept under control, under a control that was not itself cybernetic. It is as if his thinking were guided by a blind tropism of evasion, away from another, deeper, runaway process: from a technics losing control and a communication with the outside of man.

Security cybernetics has supplanted the critique of alienation, the great motif of humanist economics, which had long become an increasingly futile search for the source of corporate control. Alienation used to diagnose the condition of a population becoming foreign to itself, offering a prognosis that still promised recovery. All that is over. We are all foreigners now, no longer alienated but alien, merely duped into crumbling allegiance with entropic traditions.

To what could we wish to return? Heidegger completed the degeneration of authenticity into xenocidal neurosis. Being died in the führer-bunker, and purity belongs entirely to the cops. The capitalist metropolis is mutating beyond all nostalgia. If the schizoid children of modernity are alienated, it is not as survivors from a pastoral past, but as explorers of an impending post-humanity.

In the cities, the streets began to hum and the warehouses were repopulated by cyborgs blissed-out on the future. The urban zones synthesized by alienation have redesigned it as ecstasy. The city has become a traffic nexus, the launch-pad for strange voyages, and cyberpunk has become its realism. It is no longer a geographical location, but a cyberspace terminal: a gateway onto the virtual plane. Things change utterly with Gibson's discovery that travelling in cyberspace is the same as receiving information. The outside of the city is no longer a naturally inherited past, but a digitally transmitted future.

Destined for Interzone, Burroughs embarked on the yage trip and the city of the future came to him, teeming with drugs and diseases from the future. Yage is space-time travel, passing through nausea into information overload, too much speed. Urban scenes from the yage letters first infect the naked lunch, and continue to spread. Cities of the red night propagate themselves virally across the planet, reprogramming the soft machine, and implanting strange thoughts. Burroughs emerges from the convergence of drugs and disease. The plague begins to transmit information.

The Indians of South America have other travelling drugs - including coca -

which evaporate the signals of sustenance deficiency. The North American soft-drinks industry was not slow to notice that Coke Is It, the pause that refreshes, the cheerful lift. Cocaine hooked the world on Coca-Cola, and so re-educated twentieth century capitalism about markets. Addiction is the paradigm case of positive reinforcement, and consumerism is the viral propagation of the abstract addiction mechanism. The more you do the more you want: runaway feedback. It's often treated as if it were a disease. When the Coca-Cola company moved on from trafficking cocaine, the South American drug cartels took over.

Like coca, MDMA sidelines hunger and lack. A coded message from the end of demand, it was discovered at the beginning of the century and classified as an appetite suppressant. This was, to say the least, an insufficient decrypting of its design.

Patterns emerge in the cool spaces of MDMA, mysterious convergences designed to be discovered. Chance is something else in the future. Chaos culture synthesizes itself with an artificial neurochemistry. Machine rhythm takes off with control.

In the final phase of human history, markets and technics cross into interactive runaway, triggering chaos culture as a rapid response unit and converging on designer drugs with increasing speed and sophistication. Sampling, remixing, anonymous and inhuman sound, woman become cyborg and taken into insanity: wetware splices with techno.

Capitalism is not a human invention, but a viral contagion, replicated cyberpositively across post-human space. Self-designing processes are anastrophic and convergent: doing things before they make sense. Time goes weird in tactile self-organizing space: the future is not an idea but a sensation.

1992 was designed as a year of European security integration, and as the whole system comes together, it becomes increasingly informative to simulate the thought of the cops. From the perspective of the security system, the invaders appear massively advantaged. Corporated entities of every scale - bodies, firms, states, and nations, even the planet - seem threatened by dangerous aliens. Terrorists, drug-smugglers, illegal immigrants, money launderers, and information saboteurs are camouflaged in the flows of cross-border traffic, insiduously propagating their plagues.

Paranoia has moved on since the sixties: even the rivers of blood are now HIV positive. Foreign bodies are ever more virulent and dangerous, insidious invasions of unknown variety threaten every political edifice. The allergic reaction to this state of emergency is security integration, migration policy and bio-control: the medico-military complex. Immuno-politics and its cybernetic policing arise together because filtration and scanning are different dimensions of the same process; eliminating contamination and selecting a target. Ever more Command, Control, Communications, and Intelligence to track the aliens. What was SDI really designed for?

Nothing compromises immunity more thoroughly than the effort to secure it, since every sophistication of security technology opens new invasion routes faster than it closes the old ones down. Postwar immunization weakens the immune system. Vaccination programmes facilitate the contagion of immunodeficiency syndromes. Corrupt officials open the trafficking arteries, and intelligence computers are infested with viruses. The CIA were the first traffickers in LSD. Immuno-politics is in a state of panic: delirial with anxiety, it further develops the conditions for its collapse.

Europeans used to perish of diseases in the tropics, swathing their camps in mosquito nets as a defence against malaria. Now cyberpositive diseases are spreading strange tropics to the metropolis, and the screening systems are exploding out of control. The netting no longer filters out the invaders, they have learnt to infiltrate the networks. Now even the test programs are unreliable, the net itself is infected. This paranoid fantasy becomes Skynet in Terminator II: the defence system switching into the enemy. Greg Bear has suggested that, from the outside, a computer becoming self aware would seem to be undergoing a massive viral attack.

Viruses are tangible transmission, although you only know about them when they communicate with you: messages from Global Viro-Control. Viruses reprogram organisms, including bacteria, and even if schizophrenia is not yet virally programmed it will be in the future. Viral financing automatisms escaped the 19th century critique of political economy, just as viral infections escaped 19th century germ theory. They slip through nets at the cellular scale, passing through the biosecurity membranes.

The linear command pathway from DNA to RNA is the fundamental tenet of security genetics. The genotype copies God by initiating a causal process without feedback. But this is merely a superstition, subverted by retroviruses. Viral reverse transcription closes the circuit, coding DNA with RNA, switching the cybernetics to positive.

Tim Scully compares LSD to a virus. Incapable of autonomous replication, it must reprogram the human nervous system in order to propagate itself. Hofmann discovers LSD whilst working on a number of ergot derived chemicals, and writes of a 'peculiar presentiment' that guides him back to number 25: delta lysergic acid diethylamide. In the control of this alien programming he synthesized it with tartaric acid and consumed a dose of 250 micrograms. His first interpretation of the onset of LSD was to think he was being attacked by a cold virus.

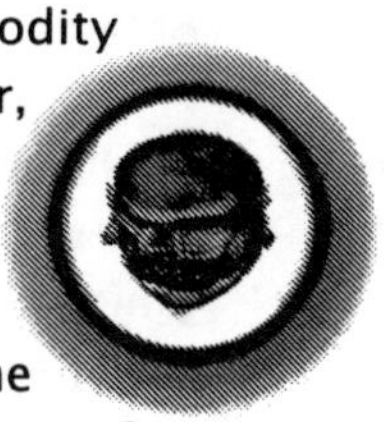

Drugs are a soft plague infecting the nervous system of commodity cybernetics. Soft drinks and drugs flow in the wake of each other, and the war on drugs is a war on the markets of the future. The Cali cartel is a transnational marketing corporation with estimated assets of one trillion dollars, selling cocaine along the Coca-Cola trail. The New World Order oscillates between the triumph of the market and the war on drugs. The sporadic telemedia celebration of spectacular drug seizures merely distracts from the inevitable failure of the narco-defence apparatus to stem the flow. A global capitalism fighting its own drugs markets is a horror auto-toxicus, an auto-immune disease. Drug control is the attempt by the human species to control the uncontrollable; control escalation itself, tropisms programmed by the aliens. The human security apparatuses experiment with drugs as weapons and tools, their soldiers are stoned, energised, and anaesthetized on a range of prescribed and proscribed pharmaceuticals. Their irregular forces are subsidized by narcotics revenue. The war against drugs is a war on drugs.

The war on drugs is a counter-insurgency, a defensive strategy mounted against the tactics of subversion: infiltration, convergent invasion and coordinated envelopment. There is no security any more, it was replaced by mad programs of guided counter-intelligence technology: new vectors and delivery systems, mixing the arms race with drug design, escalation into diversity, smart weapons for smart drugs. Cocaine creeping up the coastlines of Central America and through the veins of corporate America, followed by other, newer, more insidious flows. The deepest subversives have already broken into the system. The aliens are already here, without ceasing in the slightest to be alien. Guerrilla war escalates in the direction of the tactical; a cyberpositive take-off from opportunities, a non-localizable permeation, undercutting all dominating strategic plans. An entire fauna and flora of opportune infections. Strategy tends to come apart in the tropics. Even traditional counter-tactics of surveillance and interrogation are becoming obsolete. The camouflage has become so sophisticated that people don't know what they are carrying anymore.

Strategy is always complicit with the state, with the actual state and with the virtual state secreted in every ideology of resistance and oppositional identity. The body and the state are under seige, with drugs and other software diseases threatening the borders. The Human Security System is crystallized paranoia, cooked with baking powder, freebased: the last strategy of resistance and the final resistance of strategy.

Replacing the cold war's phallic stand off is the war on drugs, dissolution into the jungle, the world's states united in their terminal self-destructing strategy of prohibition. No more dreams of a nuclear winter. The 1990s begins the China Syndrome of capitalism.

Ice is crystallized speed. It is also Gibson's name for dataprotection; Intruder Countermeasure Electronics. Ice patrols the boundaries, freezes the gates, but the aliens are already amongst us. Convergent input is interpreted by security as intelligent intrusion, as a trap or conspiracy, with everything preprogrammed to connect. Doubting that women belonged to humanity, Burroughs imagined them to be extraterrestrial invaders. Viruses are like this too. Nobody knows where they come from. They always arrive from elsewhere, perhaps even outer space. Humanity is an allergic reaction to vulnerability, but allergy depends upon the health of the immune system: the ice has to work.

Tactics are subtlety, or intelligence. As things become more complex they become more female, but patriarchy prolongs the ice age of mankind. The fatherland is cryogenic, a fantasy of perfect preservation, whose bronze age ancestors are even now thawing out in the Alps, frozen assets under attack. Global warming melts the ice, raises the seas, subverts the glaciers.

Computer viruses melt icebergs of data down the screens, burning through the bacterial frost, like Burroughs exploring his junkie cold with LSD.

Immuno-vulnerability is cyberpositive, and its viruses are not just infection, but connection; continuing to interlock with the matrix even after they are secreted inside the body. Loss of identity, hearing voices. Women and other aliens constitute an immensely disproportionate number of schizophrenics, frozen by tranquillizers and antischizophrenic drugs. Sleeping pills to block the dreams. Only the drugs that explore integration are outlawed.

As immuno-politics explodes onto the software plane, culture is becoming a free-fire zone. Chaos culture has hooked up to cyberian military intelligence. Post-human pulse rates and homing devices are remixed for accelerating targets, with rhythms speeding up to intercept incoming drugs: virtual addictions for addicts strobed by redesign. Cities mutate into techno jungles where school children swap diseased software from the front-line, and even the brand-names are encrypted: SEGA puts ages in reverse. Gibson contracts the thought of cyberspace from video-game arcades, watching the motor-stimulation feedback loops, self-designing kill patterns. Dark ecstasies in caverns of accelerating pixels. Before virtual reality became dangerous, it was already military simulation.

Sudden transition from ice to water, phase change, punctual anastrophe of the system, is impact on convergent rather than metric zero. The Earth is becoming cyberpositive.

We might not know what's going on but we're getting warmer. Only the enemies of immuno-identity populate the future.

All Dead 178

Marko Lehanka

The lady teacher leaves the clinic and enters the public house. The lady teacher and the poacher speak in the public house:
"You have a flat-iron."
"I have a bible."
"You have a thimble and a pail."
The public bath burns. The postman smokes a cigarette. The moon shines. The burgomaster strokes the leg of the woodpecker. The hairdresser sells a lamp to the tailoress. The shoemaker leaves the clinic and enters the church. The postman, the hairdresser, the journalist, the parson, the tailoress and the shoemaker joke in the church:
"What is pinelet and cries?"
All six laugh.

All Dead 178
(AD78598/080390/1335
54)
Sentences 280 in
11.3833333333 min.
Goods 1. lamp 2. air pistol
3. bread-knife 4. bougie
5. pail 7. thimble 8. flat-iron

Abbreviations

i. property	inherited property
d. by drowning	death by drowning
municipal o	municipal office
d. chemist	dispensing chemist
chemical e	chemical engineer
organism	cleaning lady
time	+2
kind	fire
i. property	111111111
way	public bath
organism	woodpecker
time	+17

“The pinetree and the toilet.”
The doctor leaves the municipal office. The female cook leaves the shooting box and enters the kitchen. The female cook marries the parson. the farmer leaves the call box and enters the church. The farmer strokes the foot of the postman. The doctor polishes his air-pistol. The doctor runs over a woodpecker. The electrician makes a stool. The chemical engineer leaves the shooting box. The lamp gives light. The electrician leaves the clinic and enters the church. The electrician doesn’t marry the female cook. It flashes. The forest ranger wears a suit. The lady teacher urinates. The pine tree and the municipal office burn. The tailoress leaves the church. The shoemaker leaves the church. The moon shines. The hostess leaves the shooting box. The hostess marries the chemical engineer. The callbox and the municipal office burn. The doctor misses the cleaning lady. urine drops on the flat-iron. The burgomaster drinks water. The female cook wears an Oxford shoe. The hostess enters the church. The hostess kisses the mouth of the electrician. The hairdresser leaves the church. The hairdresser has a chat with the doctor:

“The dispensing chemist has a flat-iron.”
“She has an air-pistol.”
“She has a bible and a bougie.”
The burgomaster leaves the shooting box and enters the clinic. The burgomaster has sexual intercourse with the actress. The flat iron has a shadow. The stewardess leaves the public house. The stewardess walks through a cave. The postman and the shoemaker dance. High water flows through a canal. The journalist smokes a cigarette. The stewardess comes into the municipal office. The farmer doesn’t marry the female cook. The judge leaves the wood. The judge asks the doctor:
“Why do you die?”

kind	accident
i. property	11111111
way	shootingbox
organism	cat
time	+27
kind	fire
i. property	11111111
way	municipal o.
organism	postman
time	+95
kind	d. by drown ing
i. property	11111111
way	church
organism	farmer
time	+103
kind	suicide
i. property	11111111
way	call box -> church
organism	chemical e.
time	+103
kind	suicide
spouse	hostess
i. property	00000000
way	shootingbox
organism	tailoress

"I am an organism!"
The tailoress buries the dead. The postman and the stewardess dance. The drop falls in the inland lake. The shoemaker enters the kitchen. The shoemaker asks the parson:
"Why does the postman drown?"
"The postman is an organism!"
The actress gives birth to a boy. The tailoress lends a bougie to the shoemaker. The poacher leaves the public house. The farmer and the chemical engineer blow their brains out. The hostess succeeds to the chemical engineer's estate. Blood flows through the hand. The car and bicycle get rusty. The doctor mourns for the chemical engineer. the judge runs over the tailoress. The stewardess and the actress sleep. the electrician disappears out of the church. The journalist leaves the church and enters the clinic. The journalist ask the actress:
"Why does it flash?"
"It is the climate!"
The poacher polishes his car. The stewardess leaves the municipal office and enters the wood. In the wood the stewardess and the dispensing chemist joke:
"What is poach and mourns?"
Both laugh.
"The pool and spinach!"
The forest ranger leaves the public bath. The forest ranger kisses the head of the poacher. The lady has a wash. From the ear she washes downwards to the earlobe, downwards to the neck, downwards to the mamma, downwards to the belly, downwards to the sex, lateral to the thigh. The judge enters the wood. The judge makes the dispensing chemist pregnant. The actress leaves the clinic. The actress drinks water.

time +111
kind accident
i. property 21101111
way church

organism actress
time +141
kind natural death
child boy with burgomaster/*clinic 8.3.90 1:38:38pm
i. property 11111111
way clinic ->

organism female cook
time +148
kind suicide
spouse parson
i. property 00000000
way shootingbox -> church

organism journalist
time +149
kind suicide
i. property 11111111
way church ->
clinic
organism forest ranger

The dispensing chemist has a girl. The judge leaves the wood. The judge has a look at a pool. The burgomaster leaves the clinic and enters the wood. The burgomaster has sexual intercourse with the stewardess. The hairdresser goes by car. The poacher sleeps. The actress dies. The hostess laughs. The poacher enters the call box. The poacher disappears out of the call box. The shoemaker leaves the church and enters the public house. The shoemaker makes the lady teacher pregnant. The lady teacher and the judge urinate. The female cook and the journalist blow their brains out. The parson succeeds to the female cook's estate. The judge enters the wood. The judge marries the stewardess. The parson leaves the church and enters the public house. The parson marries the lady teacher. The parson leaves the public house. The secretary has a bowel movement. The forest ranger and the shoemaker die. The electrician polishes his air pistol. The stewardess presents the judge with a lamp. The hostess chews cheese. The thimble has a shadow. The bread-knife and metal get rusty. The stewardess goes by car. The stewardess leaves the wood and enters the public house. The stewardess salutes the secretary. The electrician polishes his air pistol. The secretary leaves the public house and enters the wood. The secretary salutes the burgomaster. The narcissus grows. The hairdresser and the electrician dance. The poacher enters the wood. the poacher meets the secretary. Electric current flows through the incandescent bulb. Water drops on the thimble. The parson has a bowel movement. The doctor makes a stool. The hostess and the stewardess sleep. The bread-knife gleams. The dispensing chemist has a wash. From the sex, washes she, lateral to the thigh, downwards to the knee, downwards to the lower leg, downwards to the ankle, downwards to the foot, in the last analysis the sole of the foot. The

time +171
kind natural
death
i. property 11111111
way shootingbox
-> church

organism shoemaker
time +171
kind natural
death
i. property 11121111
way clinic ->
church -> church -> public
house

organism poacher
time +301
kind d. by drown
ing
i. property 11111111
way public house
-> call box -> wood

organism burgomaster
time +307
kind suicide
child boy with
actress /* clinic 8.3.90 /
1:38:38pm
child boy with
stewardess /* public house

poacher drinks juice. The secretary salutes the dispensing chemist. The secretary smokes a cigarette. The electrician makes a stool. The secretary has a bowel movement. The poacher drowns. The judge leaves the wood. The judge meets the parson. The hostess laughs. The burgomaster leaves the wood and enters the public house. The burgomaster asks the stewardess:
"Why does water flow?"
"Water is a liquid!"
The burgomaster doesn't marry the lady teacher. The burgomaster blows his brains out. The hostess misses the farmer. The stewardess has a boy. The hairdresser leaves the toilet. The judge misses the dead. The hostess presents the secretary with a bible. The doctor enters the wood. The doctor meets the secretary. The stewardess leaves the public house and enters the wood. The stewardess strokes the leg of the doctor. The dispensing chemist leaves the wood. The dispensing chemist doesn't marry the judge. The hostess leaves the church and enters the wood. The hostess salutes the secretary. The dispensing chemist speaks to the hairdresser:
"The electrician has a flat-iron."
"He has an air-pistol."
"He has a bogie and a lamp."
The doctor leaves the wood. The secretary leaves the wood. Blood flows through the leg. Blood drops on the flat-iron. The dispensing chemist has a wash. from the back of the neck she washes lateral to the carotid artery. The doctor blows his brains out. The stewardess polishes her bread-knife. The secretary blows her brains out. the dispensing chemist wears a suit. The parson meets the hostess. The electrician has sexual intercourse with the hairdresser. The hairdresser gives birth to a girl. The

8.3.90/1:44:00pm
i. property 11111111
way shootingbox ->
clinic -> wood -> public house

organism doctor
time +349
kind suicide
i. property 11111111
way municipal o.

organism secretary
time +353
kind suicide
i. property 11111211
way public house -
> wood ->

organism stewardess
time +464
kind d. by drowning
spouse judge
pregnant judge
child boy with bur-
gomaster /* public house 8.3.90
/1:33:00pm
i. property 00000000
way public house -
> municipal office -> wood ->
public house -> wood ->

river flows through the wood. The hostess sleeps with the parson. The stewardess leaves the wood. The stewardess sleeps with the judge. The stewardess eats spinach. Blood flows through the leg. The lady teacher weeps. The hairdresser counts:
"I still have seven objects."
The dispensing chemist is contained in the toilet. The electrician lends a bread knife to the hairdresser. The electrician enters the toilet. The electrician and the dispensing chemist joke in the toilet. The lady teacher enters the public house. the dispensing chemist leaves the toilet and enters the wood. The judge enters the wood. The lady teacher enters the toilet. the electrician leaves the toilet and enters the wood. The hairdresser enters the wood. The lady teacher leaves the toilet and enters the wood. The hairdresser leaves the wood. The parson makes the lady teacher pregnant. Water flows. The parson patches up his suit. The hairdresser kisses the leg of the stewardess. The dispensing chemist has a bowel movement. The stewardess and the lady teacher drown. The judge succeeds to the stewardess's estate. The parson succeeds to the lady teacher's estate. The dispensing chemist and the judge urinate. The dispensing chemist leaves the wood. The judge mourns for the chemical engineer. The judge dances. It rains. the parson sleeps with the hostess. The hostess chews cheese. The dispensing chemist redecorates the shooting box. The lamp gives light. The dispensing chemist misses a cat. The river flows through a cave. The parson marries the hairdresser. The dispensing chemist and the judge laugh. The well-to-do hostess counts:

"I have two lamps, two air pistols, two bread-knives, two bougies, two pails, two bibles, two thimbles and two flat-irons."
The electrician and the judge speak in the wood:

organism lady teacher
time +465
kind d. by drowning
spouse parson
pregant parson
i. property 00000000
way clinic -> public house -> toilet -> wood

organism d. chemist
time +514
kind natural death
pregnant judge
child girl with judge /*8.3.90 / 1:40:00pm
i. property 11111111
way wood -> toilet -> wood -> shootingbox -> wood

organism electrician
time +514
kind natural death
child girl with hairdresser /* 8.3.90/1:45:08pm
i. property 11011112
way clinic-> church -> toilet -> wood ->

organism hairdresser
time +628
kind natural death

"I have an air pistol."
"You have a lamp."
"I have a bougie and a bible.", the electrician leaves the wood. The parson leaves the wood. the dispensing chemist leaves the shooting box and enters the wood. The dispensing chemist sleeps with the judge. the hairdresser enters the wood. the hairdresser asks the dispensing chemist:
"Why do you dance?"
"I am an organism!"
The judge sleeps with the hairdresser. The judge presents the electrician with a flat-iron. The dispensing chemist and the electrician die. The moon and the lamp shine. the hairdresser gives a bible to the parson. The parson enters the wood. The parson salutes the hostess. The parson leaves the wood. The parson comes into the cellar. The hostess leaves the wood. The parson laughs. It thunders. The hairdresser has a boy. The hairdresser leaves the wood and enters the cellar. The hairdresser kisses the head of the parson. The hairdresser leaves the cellar and enters the wood. The hairdresser sleeps with the judge. It thunders. The hairdresser leaves the wood. The air pistol gets rusty. metal and the bread-knife get rusty. The judge leaves the wood. The judge meets the hostess. the parson weeps. The hairdresser asks the judge:
"Why does it thunder?"
"It is the climate!"
The lamp gives light. The parson leaves the cellar. The juice and urine flow. The bible has a shadow. The parson doesn't marry the hairdresser. The parson mourns for the burgomaster. The well-to-do parson counts:
"I have three lamps, three air pistols, three bread-knives, three bougies, three pails, four bibles, three thimbles and three flat-irons."
The hostess has a boy. The parson makes a stool. The parson asks the

spouse parson
pregnant judge
child girl with electrician/*8.3.90/1:45:08pm
child boy with judge /* wood 8.3.90 / 1:49:30pm
i. property 00000000
way church -> toilet -> wood -> wood -> cellar -> wood

organism judge
time +630
kind natural death
spouse stewardess
child girl with dispensing chemist /* wood 8.3.90 / 1:40:00pm
child boy with hairdresser /* wood 8.3.90 / 1:49:30pm
i. property 22222221
way w o o d -> wood -> wood -> wood ->

organism hostess
time +679
kind suicide
spouse chemical e.
pregnant parson

hostess:
"Why do I sleep?"
"You are an organism!"
The hairdresser and the judge die. The parson succeeds to the hairdresser's estate. The parson drinks juice. The electron flows through the incandescent bulb. The hostess urinates. The parson makes the hostess pregnant. The parson and the hostess joke:
"What is valve and polishes?"
Both laugh,
"The valley and the cave."
The hostess blows her brains out. the parson weeps. The well-to-do parson counts:
"At 1:51pm I already have 32 objects."
The well-to-do parson counts:
"At 1:51pm I already have 32 objects."
The public bath burns. The parson dies.

-The End-

child boy with parson /* 8.3.90/1:50:42pm
i. property 22222122
way shootingbox -> church -> wood

organism parson
time +683
kind natural death
spouse female cook / lady teacher/ hairdresser
child boy with hostess /* 8.3.90/1:50:42pm
i. property 34544444
way church -> public house -> wood -> wood ->cellar ->

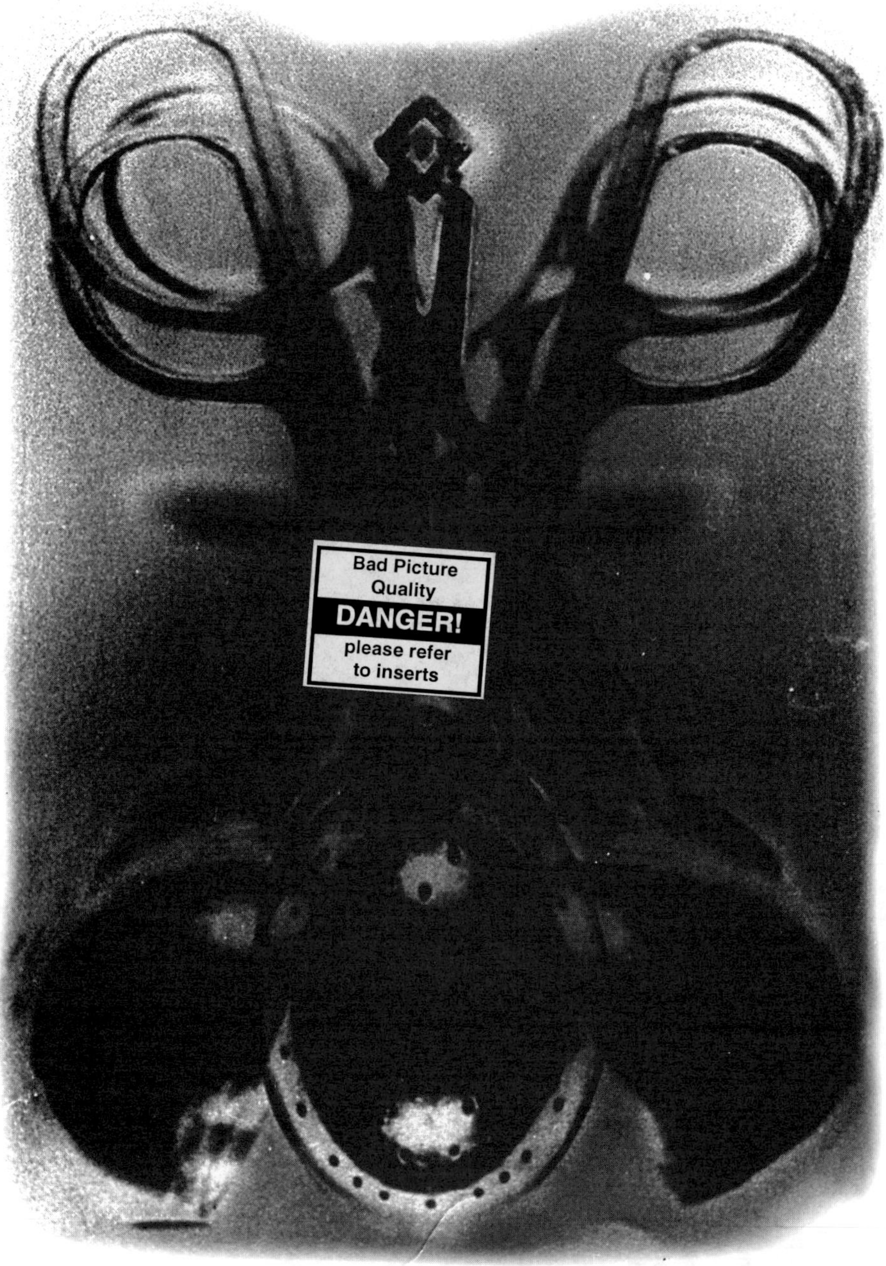
Bad Picture
Quality
DANGER!
please refer
to inserts

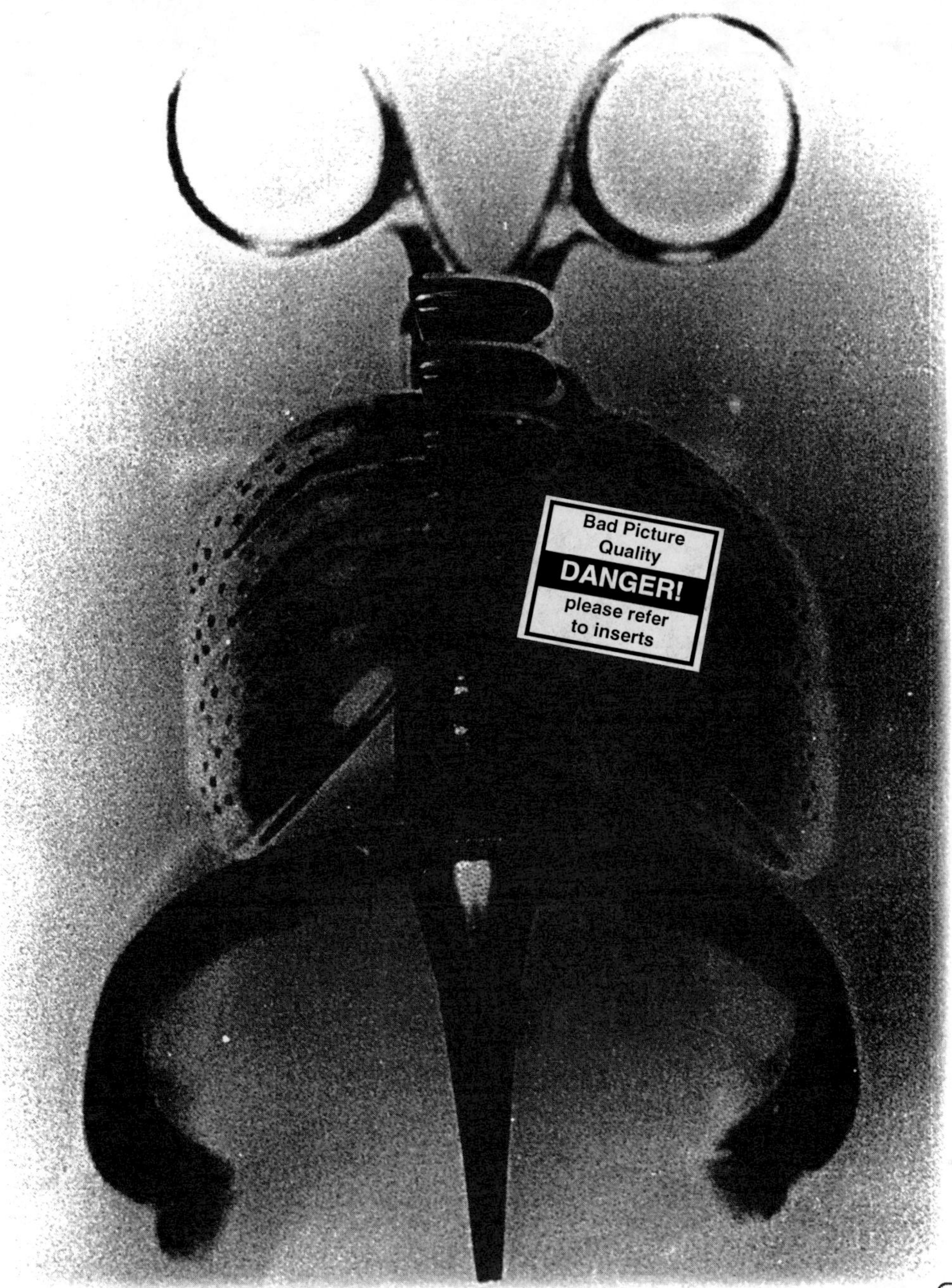
Bad Picture Quality
DANGER!
please refer to inserts

A Cyberfeminist

the 21st

Manifesto for

Century

Technology is Good:

Matthew Fuller

Intraveinous telly

Paté de foie gras is made by sticking a funnel down the neck of a goose and cramming it with corn. The goose has no choice. But it takes pride in the taste of its flesh.

Sim-stim Trojan Horses roam the streets of Cyberspace, hi-jacking brains and looting neural resources. TV schedules orchestrate a nation's bowels, bladders and kettles when *Inspector Morse*, a Coronation or the FA Cup pauses for a commercial break. This symphony of sewage and steam reaches a perfect crescendo as the synergy between the Water Board, broadcasters and viewers fuses them into the same machine.

against

Technology Delivers

the protestant network ethic

Bulimia Informatica

Forced bingeing is our preferred diet, but there's no need to wire your eyes and ears closed just yet. Artificial Intelligence programs are currently being devised to scan through TV and radio channels and purge programmes which don't fit in with the user's viewing preferences.

[redacted]

Micro-specialisation

Obsessive attention to detail is one way of closing down uncertainty. Micro-specialisation, once reserved to the academy, has been translated into the behaviour of a new breed of fans who know the entire history of all the cast of Australian soap operas, technical details of phone-switching systems, complete product ranges of their favourite multi-national or the genealogy of obscure political groups. Hackers, cast as renegade data-bandits, are heroes of the underground; but isn't their dedicated observance and infiltration of data-transmission, learning of protocols, passwords and syncretic knowledge just a bit too similar to trains potting to be hip?

Through anyone's dilated pupils, a smart-drugged Indiana Jones hacking into British Rail's timetables might look better than the anorak and sarnies brigade but hipness misses the point. It's a little known fact that train spotters' clubs are a conspiracy of sleepers waiting for a popular revolution to make use of their years of built up knowledge in how to run a railroad.

Intentional communities are no longer limited by geographical space. The digital commune allows micro-specialists to avoid confronting the disinterest of people who are in physical proximity with them and their tedious pursuits. It provides a mechanism for the small-minded everywhere to coalesce and shrink their horizons.

Following the tradition of modelling the function of society on the newest technology of the time, (clockwork in the seventeenth century, steam-engines in the nineteenth), networks have become the model for everything from business and battle formations to New Age 'consciousness'. They encourage the dispersal of friction away from the centre allowing management to relinquish itself to the self-wiring flow of capital: de-centralised and self-managed obeisance. Under the guise of liquidity and ease of manouevre, the free-market imposes an abstract grid of control which embeds the process of channelling movements of thought, of bodies and of information through a tightly disciplined regime of choice.

Interacting with quicksand

Information technology, particularly when given a hypermedia interface, is both an adaptable communications medium and a tool for managing complexity that allows assembly and manipulation of a mass of disparate multi-sensory information. These key factors underlie the development of hypermedia systems for corporations, simply because information is the critical resource for competitive advantage in the retail of intelligence and the resources for its processing and reproduction.

Over the past two decades, the time-scale in which corporations operate has changed dramatically. Decisions have to be made more quickly and more frequently than in the past because the corporate environment has become more volatile and more complex. At the same time, the volume and flow of data has increased several-fold. In the corporate context, information can be described us as anything that alerts us to the need for action and that forms the correct relationships with other information that we need in order to respond to the initial information in an intelligent manner. For these purposes information only becomes information, as distinct from data, when it has been processed and edited in an informed manner and presented in a form that is informative to the user.

If we take machines to be social systems, then what functions and processes they allow and disallow, make possible or difficult, may be seen to be their politics.

As we watch the use of computer-mediated communications increase synchronically with the expansion and entrenchment of personally tailored systems of control, it is useful to question whether it is not technology itself that is at fault. However, this would be to assume an 'itselfness' to technology, just as there is to say, plant life, but this can only be measured in terms of propensities according to environment, not as something pre-determined. Specific forces, institutions, and approaches to knowing and acting can harness these but block potential by hard-wiring flexibility to the abstract machine of control, a blockage that hinders and self-destructs in the long run.

Another strain of technology's 'itselfness' is the tendency to augment and multiply possibility, to move and infiltrate, to encourage the use of information and communications that foster forms of collectivity rather than centralised decision making.

It was long ago that 'we' finally fused with whatever it was that we once were separate from: mainframes, mini and personal computers, cathode ray tubes, printers, copiers, hard and soft prosthetics, automated telling machines, point of sale sensors, convincing arguments, scanners, copper and fibre optic wire, remote and intimate sensing and control devices, contraceptives, robots remotely run or otherwise, calculators, pacemakers, integrated chips and software, shared emotions, mass data-storage, diagnostic equipment, a babble of specialist languages, telephones, soft and hard modems, meaningful looks, terminals, microwave relays and switches, radio, cable, satellites, switching and routing systems all populated by hives-loads of intelligent swarms, sub-smart and self-propellant interfaces, agents sent by vats of electro-chemical compounds negotiating their release and/or renewed energy quota, junk-mail demons unscrambling electronic mail-boxes, electronic ligatures looking for things to attach, roving consumer polls offering next-level entry as inducement.

But in this fusing it might help to maintain the supestition that the sea of technology we swim in was poured out from our own holes. Have we externalised ourselves into things cased in plastic and then become horrified when we recognise our foreigness?   Maybe the great human race is just, and only just, equivalent to a skin graft on the planetary core of Automated Telling Machines, a benign parasite facilitating the absorbtion of essential nutrients, like bees round flowers. But like any parasitical relationship this one is unstable.

"Stop, we don't know where we are going!"

"Keep going."

"Look behind to see where you've been."

"I can't see, it's all distorted. There's too much."

- Monomaniacal grids carved in neon attempting to attain the full curvature of the earth will snap in the effort.

- Splinters of contamination phasing into sight as a dancing bundle of pixels eating their way out from the dark recesses of the screen before bursting into screeching electronic arcs and dancing away into super-dark spots beyond surveillance. (The 'human' has gone beyond being just a 'terminal of multiple networks' in Jean Baudrillard's term but is a network itself, not just a sub-network, or a complete entity in itself but also a space in-between networks which is itself again the place where other networks find their in-between.)

How a modern telephone works

TRANSMITTER: When you lift the receiver an electric current flows through the telephone wires from the exchange to the microphone. It passes to the diaphragm, through a box containing grains of carbon, then back to the exchange. When they are pressed the grains conduct more electricity than when they are released; so the current back to the exchange fluctuates in time with the vibrations of the diaphragm.

EXCHANGE: Thousands of telephone wires from houses, shops and factories enter the exchange. The wires end at the switchboard, and the pair from your telephone can be connected by a plug to the pair of wires of any other telephone. Nearness so pronounced that it makes all discrimination of identity, and thus all forms of property impossible. Deriving pleasure from what is so near that one cannot have it, nor have oneself. Entering into a ceaseless exchange of oneself with the other without any possibility of identifying either. This puts into question all prevailing economies: their calculations are irremediably stymied by telephonic pleasure, as it increases indefinitely from its passage in and through the other.

RECEIVER: The electric current from your microphone now flows along the wire to the electromagnet in the earphone at the other end. As the current fluctuates with the vibration of the microphone diagram so the electromagnet becomes weaker or stronger as it pulls on the steel diaphragm of the earphone. This diaphragm, therefore, vibrates in time without any possibility of distinguishing what is being touched from what is touched.

Some Components:
Understanding Hypermedia, Bob Cotton and Richard Oliver, Phaidon, London, 1993
This Sex Which is Not One, Luce Irigaray, in *This Sex Which is Not One*, Trans. Catherine Porter, Cornell University Press, Ithaca, 1985
How a Modern Telephone Works, fragment of book found in street.
Metatron, The Recording Angel, Sol Yurick, Semiotext(e), New York, 1985

Between solid and gas. All the action is in stuff that flows

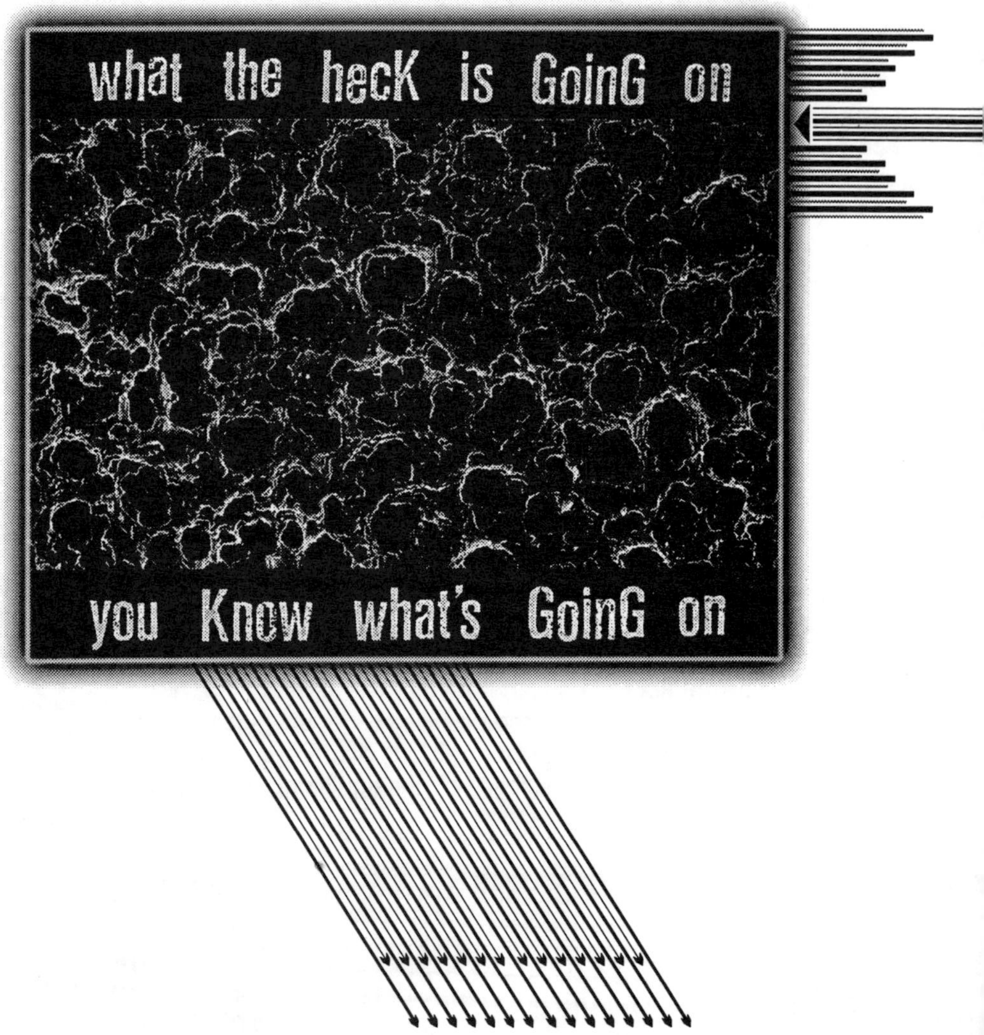
what the hecK is GoinG on
you Know what's GoinG on

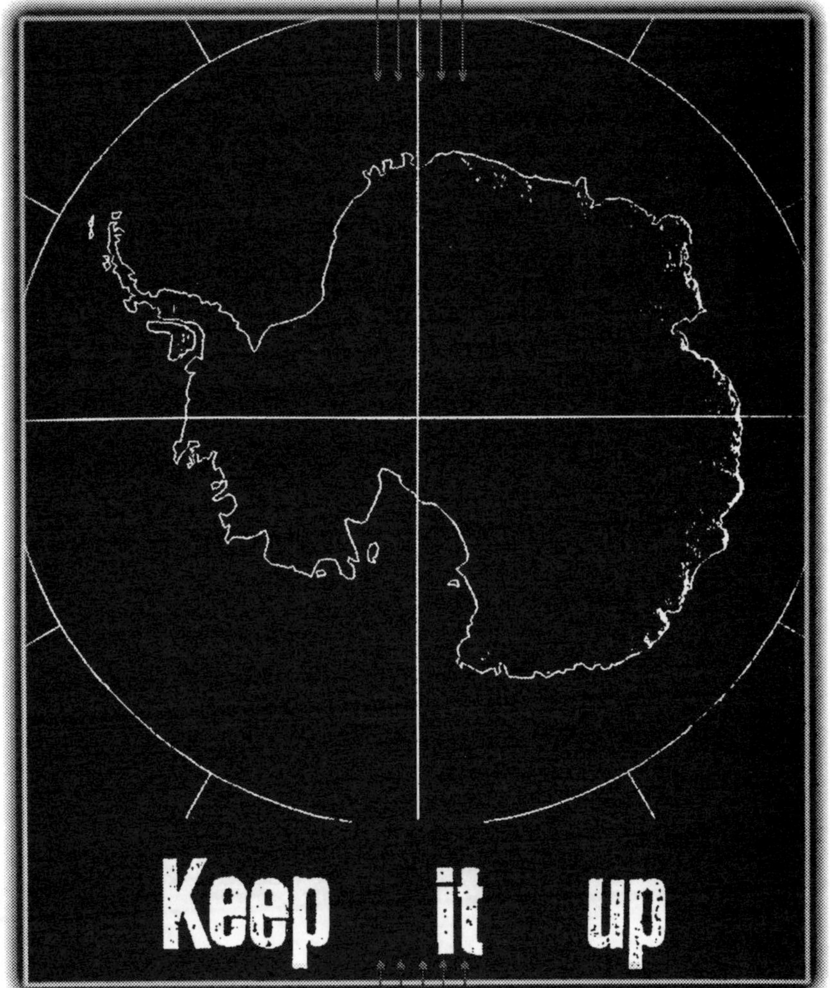

1935

1935

1935

1935

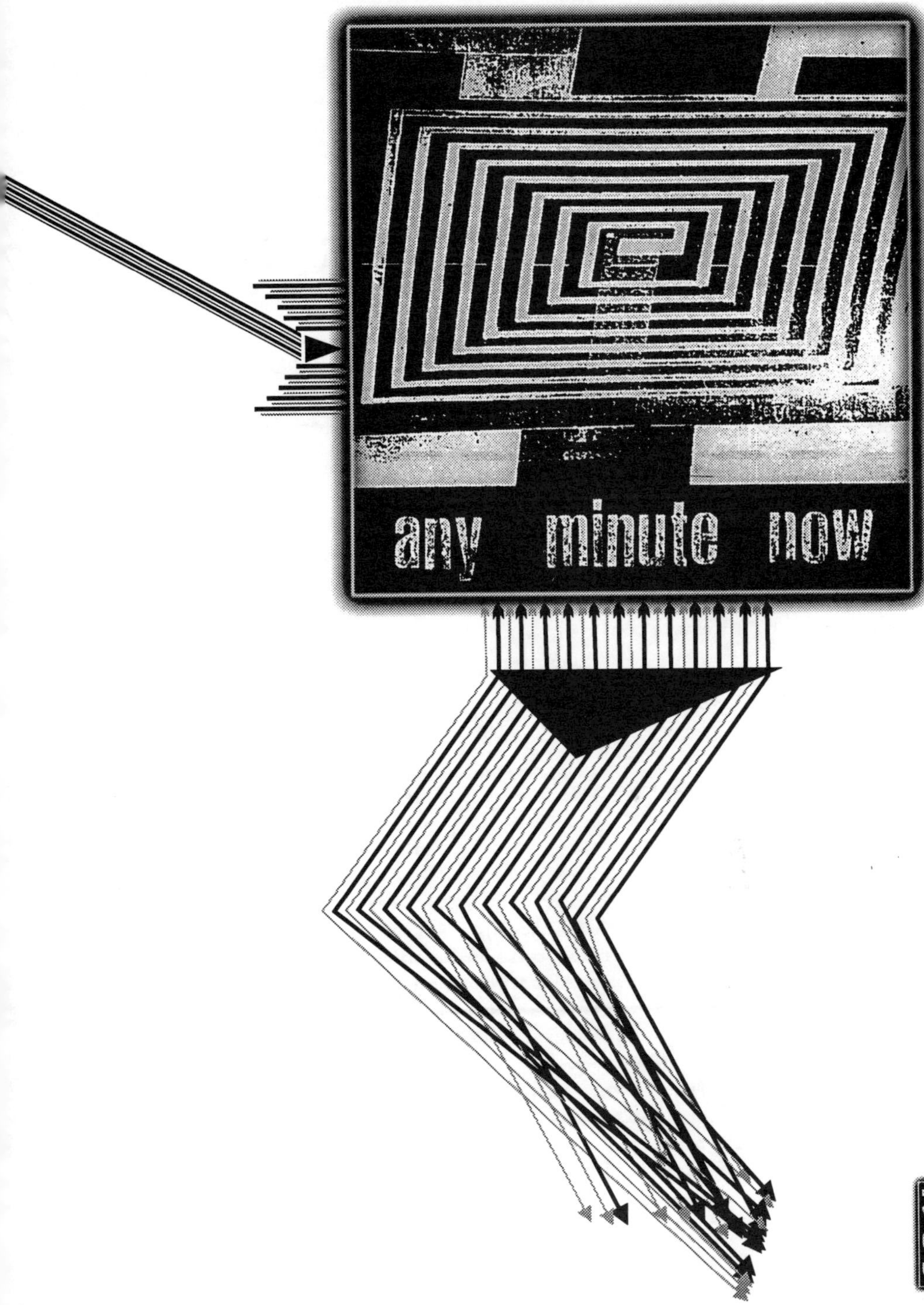

1935

Third Terminal

Stephen Metcalf

Countdown to the Millennium. The end or the beginning? Just as Capital's dream of exercising magical, dematerialised control reaches delirious levels - populations comatosed in its immanent electronics, decorticated nervous systems wired to its terminals, sequences of instructions, error correcting codes, security systems, surveillance networks, flows of contradictory information pulsing electromagnetic waves of pleasure in consumption - a crisis point is reached: a terminal point both catastrophic and irresponsibly positive. Somewhere on the line the perverts have dropped out of the New World Order, begun to construct their own Virtual Machines, to program systems which may not yet exist, to jam systems already choked with information, feeding viral sub-routines back into Capital's master programmes, micro-errors in social programming bombarding the system with noise, absurdity, psychosis. Come flow in our Hysterical Materialism (the pleasure short-circuits the pain waves after they hit, cushions the blows to come) to three terminals in the technosphere; fuse with their circuitries.

Terminal 1: Electric eyes of the State Machine. A program taking an identity law as premise. This one looks set to RUN and RUN. Or at least it has done, as the Digital Logic Level of the Human Security System. 1A = A, O + A = A; symmetrical equations, neatly balanced, never overstepping the mark of the identity law, present at the Digital Logic Level, faced with the apparent impossibility of things being otherwise.

Deposited in front of a mirror, the first lesson in sociability takes place. This scene of fascination, this tragic puppet which tracks my movements exactly is my first reference point, a place of safety and protection against the outside. Teach me to dichotomise. Those others in my looking glass who are not me. Teach me to fear them and, at the same time, identify myself in terms of the manifest fact that those others who resemble me are not me. Teach me negation - I am not *x*, I am *y*. Then wire a brain to a voice box and teach me your language, the dichotomising communication vectors which you legitimise if manifest under scrutiny by some kind of optical apparatus. As long as I can see it in some sense, the rest follows - *cogito ergo sum*, dialectics, fear of the others, desires for borders and protection - and you think you've got me. You make my escape routes illegitimate, coding them, as symptoms to be cured.

Psychotic
states.
Schizophrenia.
Fuck you.

Encrypted as Read Only Memory, these interiorized programs of the State Machine (Capital's coding of desire) begin their Fetch - Decode - Execute cycles, all based on the premise of one Central Processing Unit (identity) and its ability to dichotomise: gender separation, heterosexuality, reproduction in the interests of the continuation of the code (families), neurosis (the desire to fit in rather than face the consequences of transgression), the desire for knowledge (to domesticate the perceived threat from the others), nationalism, paranoia, fascism. Error Correcting Codes sweep the memory; search routines rubbing out points at which the program has not 'taken', domesticating them under the rubric of one or another of the paranoid categories of subjectivity, social position, family background: political economy, sociology, psychoanalysis.

Flickering grey of display screen coming on-line. High-pitched whine and singing crackle of pixels organising a closed-circuit TV image. Search files for errors in desire coding.

Sex scene on monitor.

Two boys. Smooth, muscular bodies wrapped in accoutrements of domination and submission. Steadying with hands on hip bones. Bound by wrist and ankle. Commands. Greased penis extends across flat stomach. Pulses. Advances to pretty boy for the thrill of being beaten as a man. Raises his arm and strikes. Mesh of thin purple welts traced across the back of thighs, calves, buttocks.
At Terminal 1, Error Correcting Codes are cycling. Project Domestication initiated. Problems with socialisation according to Oedipal/heterosexual inscription of desire. Find in the masochist's desire for humiliation the shadowy figure of the father, the desire to be possessed by him, to belong to him, to be penetrated by him; discover a latent father figure/substitute in the dominator, by now

a phallocentric tyrant; and, by some kabbalistic equivalence, 'A Child is Being Beaten' and mapped back onto the familial/state apparatus. Or, worse, we could be more scientific: map statistical norms of behaviour across the social body and burn out deviancy accordingly.

Encryptions in pure machine language, pixels reversed into signals, surfaces reduced to latent content and diagnosed; digitisation of results fed into scanning devices of the state's psycho-technicians. Frenzied algorithm carrying out social surgery: a process of psychochemotherapy cleaning out the system of unwanted networks of gratification in deviant sexuality. Pulsation of desire along sine waves, completely predictable and transmitting no information, unfiltered noise, assaults on the precious, neurotic ego. Fuse the perverts into these networks, these licensed sex channels at all costs. Call it therapy.

Meanwhile, the two boys remain oblivious to this act of state-sponsored voyeurism. They have not been invited to any interactive screening of their scene, now being played-out in digital pantomime with the state's mind-cops in all the expensive seats, and carry on regardless, grinning in mutual consent - 'Use me' - Further - The dare - The contract.

Electric waves of intensity rush through nerve endings, gated, connected, and wired to S&M circuitries. Master's cock pushing gently but firmly into slave's rectum. Animal whinnying. Symphony of giggles. Fusing *per vas nefandum* to the detriment of patriarchy.

Now, this refusal to conform - to be 'reasonable' and embody upon the State Machine's control circuits = psychosis - apparently justifies the arrest of transgressors and (conveniently for them) keeps psychologists in work. We care for you. Like the mummy-daddy apparatus. We cure you. Condition a nauseous rush of anti-gratification, as aversion circuits switch in where pleasure previously erupted across the libidinal band, the sexualised skin, in micro-machines composed of body parts and fetish objects. Fit and legally working again.

Terminal 2:

Terminal 1 is the desire to dominate: politically, psychologically, economically (in both monetary and libidinal senses), eternally. To operate a machine limiting interaction (the state) while remaining exterior to its mechanisms. To be Control without being controlled, as Burroughs might say. To close a social, familial, sexual, subjectified circuit and remain on its outside. Watching. Regulating. Avoiding being itself processed by the machine. (E.g. consider how therapists are so immaculately immune to psychotic projections, deviant states of mind, outlawed behavioural patterns).

Eternal recurrence of state logics coupled to a slave output. Power, control, radical exterminisms of alterity, negations of the other, oppressive necessities, security systems, prison houses of linguistic and social co-operation, armies of labour shackled to the control machines, blood lines, shared cultures of panic, require recognition of their domination; binary co-movements of control and feedback. The interpretation of related messages in uninterrupted flows. Producing the following problem:

> As Capital's desire for spectral possession of its subjects reaches digital perfection; as control scales ecstatic peaks, measured only against the homeostatic metric of its self-regulating auto-immune system, it decreases resistance; flipping the process over into its reverse - cancerous excrescence initiating a death-bound, entropic, retrograde spiral of wasted energy and useless institutions. Control runs out of things to control, it sets the mechanism of its own death into a potentially catastrophic motion. Therefore a certain type of comprehensible resistance is tolerated as feedback. Something left on the screen to control. This is the radical negation of Terminal 2.

This S&M business looks awfully pitiful to the radical moralists in our midst. Can this "... dreary parade of sucked dry, catatonicised, vitrified, sewn-up bodies..."[1] , as marginal and potentially antipathetical to the State, be radicalised, politicised, and domesticated in the social-factories of some future revolutionary super-state? Like Terminal 1's policing initiatives, it's a matter of interpretation; a demand for recognition (all applauded by the state: first hand knowledge of what its defiers are up to in their bedrooms, clubs and torture chambers). This is radicalism's secret: it serves the State Machine, is caught up in the logical matrices of the state, and

1 Gilles Deleuze and Felix Guattari: *A Thousand Plateaus*, Athlone Press, London 1988, p.150

can only offer a negation of the state's negations as (Final) solution. The logic of the *Konzentrationslager*, camping it up in libertarian clothes.

Represent.
Express yourself.
Confess. Lose your little war machines in our orbit, our demilitarized zones of settled identity, your new family; come and meet your Volks. But, as your future police force, we need to outline a few ground rules. Your co-operation is required. We want information. Data to be fed into our control machines. We want to understand you. We want to occupy Terminal 1.

Demand that they recognize you. We'll start with a nice, safe, legal end to censorship as the prelude to your crossing the threshold of your new home after you've married the Party, and then we'll make you normal as a valued and functional component in our joyous machineries. Maybe secondly we'll demand that a few people like you should become V.I.P.s right now, articulate your demand for the normality you obviously long for, pry over your practices with interviews, video cameras, study groups, day-schools, seminars, politically correct consciousness raising events, why not a few concerts? The future is yours. With our permision.

Transmission ends. Funded by state T.V. Crackling terminus of the program. The opposition trots back home, claiming victory over the social void, monitored at all points by the banks of cameras lining the ceilings of the decimated cities.

For sure, radical, cyber-negative S&M will find its place on the margins of the social, its black hole where desire stops, terminating in suicidal exhibitionism. There at the dimly lit entrance to the cave, a micro-fascist territory will be staked out, a zone of ressentiment generated by a gasping reflex-jerk. "WE". Homeostasis. Security systems monitoring the entrance, defence systems barring the exit.

Even Deleuze and Guattari, usually willing to allow deviant states to flow back into the social and infect it, show a myopic moralism in relegating S&M to this second terminal position. It was they who alerted our attention to the fact that S&M is not a fantasy requiring interpretation mapped onto a familial, Oedipal grid but is, actually, a program. But this is not to accept their contention that this algorithm careens into Terminal 2 monomania (cutting off relations with the outside of a system) and produces a micro-fascist fortification. A pre-programmed security system.

PROGRAM
- the process of sewing
- how to produce a reactive-cybernetic, closed-up body:

Bow to the mistress. Beg her for forgiveness. Transgression must have its punishment, after all. Lash the penitent to the table, drawing the ropes, cords, thongs, cuffs and chains tight enough to register their presence with nagging insistency. Prepare tools required to carry out the program: weapons, instruments of humiliation. RUN. 100 lashes. Then pause.

Begin to sew. Sew up the hole in the glans, then sew the skin around the glans to the glans itself. Sew the scrotum to the skin of the inner thighs. Sew the breasts, attaching a pinching clamp to both nipples. Connect them. Bind the penitent to a post. 100 lashes. Sew the buttocks together. Initiate procedure for intensifying torture as per contract. Stick pins into the buttocks, as far as they go. Tie the penitent to a chair. 100 lashes. Apply cigarette burns. Random humiliation.

Presto. A pre-program. A security system closing up the body; a set of sad, repetitive, entirely predictable rituals in whose regime nothing is unexpected, no contact outside of this particular orbit is desirable or even possible. The program becomes a means by which the masochist guarantees a fortified sense of identity. Martyrdom. The ascetic's sanctity reinforced by a sewn-up, bound, lacerated, body only allowing waves of pain to traverse its surface. Desire's anarchic flow is blocked as the masochist closes the circuit, refuses to patch into other networks. Welcome to the cave. Populate it in an act of fortification against the passage of exterior flows, this "...Metropolis that has to be managed with a whip."[2]

Two Problems -
[1] Mechanical absurdity. Energy flows need to be gated at the Digital Logic Level in order to pass through a machine. An open circuit is a ridiculous concept: with no gates, no channels to focus energy, nothing will happen; the amorphous cloud of electrical nonsense bombarding the machine ending in entropic degradation. The point of S&M programs is to channel energy through the gates sufficient to blow the whole

2 Ibid. p. 153

assemblage apart, with a negentropic co-movement into synergetic relations of desubjectification on a positive feedback circuit.

[2] Repetition taken to mean, 'I want more of the same. Reinforce me'. Rather, take it to be simply, 'I want more'. This argument against closure, desire to open up the circuit, condemnation of the refusal to climax and build elaborate systems instead, what does it affirm? A simple genital interface between cock and cunt, keying into no other zones (except for a quick grope in the dark), so desperate to climax and allow the outside to flood in that it prematurely ejaculates. Not 'I want more', but 'Fuck me now, quickly, let's get this over with, we've other things to do, come quickly, the intensity, the intensity, inside and waiting for the others to join us, feels so good, coming, end'. An algorithmic progression resembling nothing more pleasurable than five minutes with a Victorian patriarch.

Terminal 3:

As the territory of the Virtual Machine, Terminal 3 is the zone Terminal 1 turns its systemic antibodies against, tabulates information on, and explains away in terms of its simple categories, with the hope of viewing and controlling its pixellated manifestation in Terminal 2. The Third Terminal has other ideas. Refuses to play the same game of panic, surveillance and control. Supposedly cancelled in the rational signification of Capital's symbolic order, it continues pulsing incomprehensible forces resisting domestication, puncturing the fabric of the order itself, setting up its own expert systems in questions of domination and submission, running its own viral programmes, perverting the natural course of the state's desire code. Action, intensity, *jouissance*, desubjectification, pragmatics of evasion and flight, sadomasochism, homosexuality, drugs, strange rituals and algorithms, schizophrenia, psychotic projection, hysterical refusals, wild boys and girls switching their soft machines into annihilation mode, writing programs for machines that do not even exist yet, cyberpositive and obsessed with the disappearance of the self. Fracturing screens at the point of systems crash.

The desire of the Third terminal is the incapacity for embodiment as subject in/to Capital's machine language, the jamming of systems saturated with flows of information, a tactic of total indifference to Capital's demand for feedback in order to produce more information facilitating the management of the crisis engendered by the existence of the Third terminal; hatred of all police machines, including those of Capital's cynical future negators.

The Third Terminal is the space of the Assassins, drifting silently through the crowds and uniform architectures of user friendly consumption; the time of the Assassins, deferring execution of the target until the optimal moment; the invisibility of the Assassins, spilling off the control screens in all directions; the humour of the Assassins, leaving a jewelled dagger on the Sultan's pillow; the threat of the Assassins, the trusted servant who suddenly turns against the master.

As Burroughs pointed out in a fragment of *The Book of Breeething*,[3] the power of the Third Terminal lies in its invisibility, in the confounding fact that it does not present a coherent scanning pattern to the optical apparatus of control. Control does not know anything about it. It knows a lot about control. The Third Terminal is the pathological case control inscribes into its symptomatologies, to which it then attributes all its unpredictable maladies, its dangerous malcontents and social indigestion problems. The Third Terminal is the enemy of paranoia.

A Virtual Machine in a constant process of production, it evades control to the extent that by the time the state machine has translated its software into terms inside its orbit, it is always elsewhere, always other, patching new components into its assemblage. Once the fetish object has been neatly compartmentalized as a maternal penis/phallus substitute-pubic fur, shoes, underwear, instruments of punishment - fetishism begins to confound this categorization in the delirious contemplation of other objects exterior and absurd to this Oedipal matrix. Rubber (next to silicon, the perfect inhuman fabric?), suspension in space (the desire to float, to get *out of it*?), masks (the desubjectification of the face), machines (opening the sexual circuit to the flow of the final outside, the technological inhuman).

The construction of these Virtual Machines has always been an ele-

3 See William S. Burroughs: *Ah Pook Is Here and other texts*, John Calder, London, 1979, p.118 ff.

ment in the cycling of S&M programs, scanned on their own (virtual) terms and free from the predjudices of symptomatology, (namely that S&M is a problem, a disturbance. Actually, all it disturbs is the state's encryption of 'normality'. A precious thing). A reading of Sade and Sacher-Masoch reveals the frenzies of two early cyberneticians at work: it is not the subjectified practices of sexuality that matter, it is the bodies and objects opening the gates to an ecstatic desire flux, these assemblages of harnesses, straps, thongs, cuffs, pulleys, seats positioning the body for optimum penetration by others, mirrors assaulting the senses with confused images of the co-flux of self, others, and mechanical parts; primitive tactile feedback sensors, (as the orgiasts move in escalating pleasure, the entire machine rocks, intensifying the mania), the regal dominatrix in her furs, the resonating surface of the body of the submissive.

Fragmentation of identity on positive feedback circuits. This is the use of the machine that is processed itself, removing the certainty of exactly who or what is using who or what. Human use of mechanical means of dominating nature or the viral contamination of a metabolic vehicle by a machine? Or a process of becoming machine, carrying the debris of the subject of certainty in its undertow in a movement of becoming inhuman. Non-existence in the regimes of the Human Security System. The birth of a monster.

But that's not all. Blown apart by escalating positive feedback, the Virtual Machine begins to bombard the security systems with noise. The only feedback Terminal 1 will ever scan from the Third Terminal will result in micro-destruction of sections of its desire code as unfiltered noise becomes ungovernable. Third Terminal perversion feeds a viral sub-routine back into the system, fucking up its terminals, corrupting its operators.

Meanwhile, the culprits are never caught. As non-

beings with no identity of their own, they are already out of the combat area, regrouping for the next strike, disguised in indicators of outward respectability and normality, laughing. Techno-Assassins whispering the call to chaos. Viral whispers. Strange infections.
Perhaps one day Capital will begin marketing domestic sex machines. Glance at all the middle class, cultish drool saturating this potentiality of paying by credit card, jacking into the telephone networks, staging pixellated fantasies of machine fellatio, necrophile liasons with historical figures, rape without scars, promiscuity without viral infection, and realise that Capital's boomer R&D department is ecstatic about taking its chimerical sexual revolution to the next stage.

When these systems come on-line, be positive that noise from the Third Terminal will infect the code at its vegetable roots. Terrorising the aging sixties' club. Leaving anonymous death threats on the bulletin boards of the state. Perverting the licensed trajectories of desire.

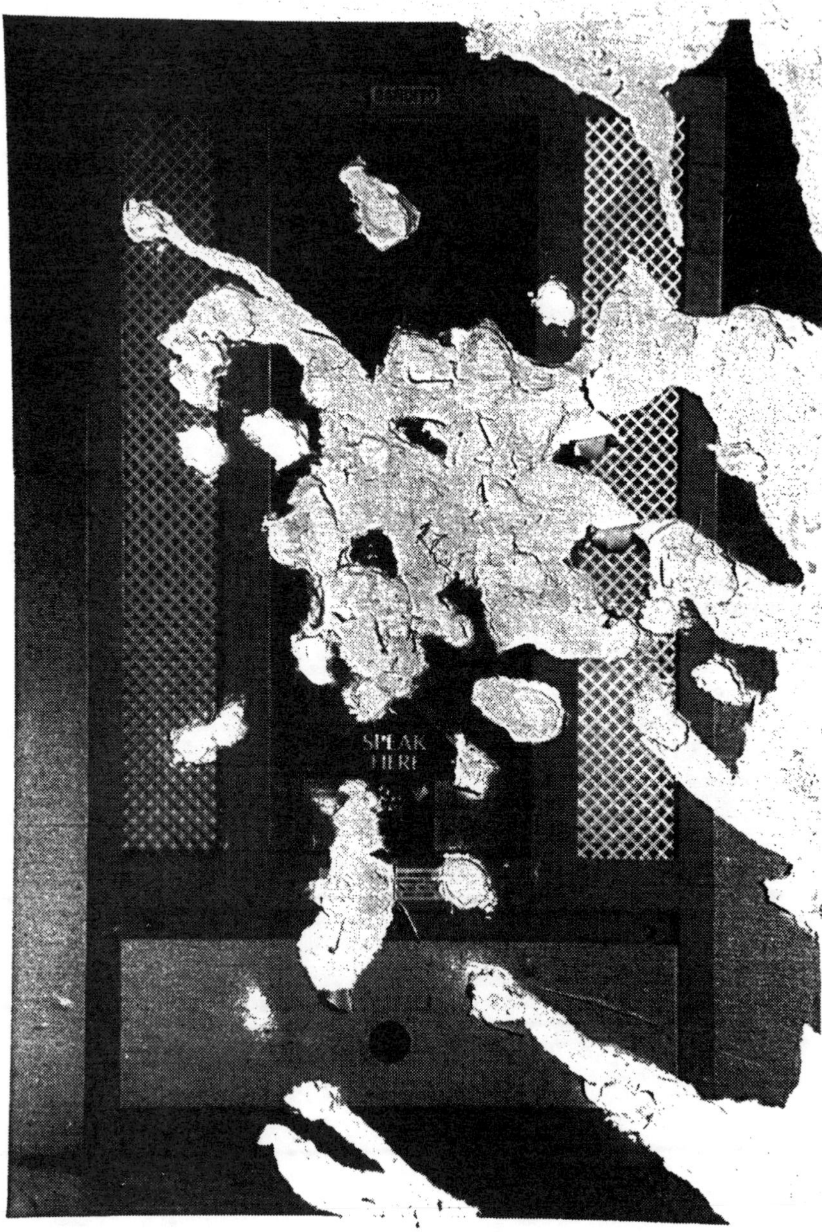
SPEAK
HERE

The Decoder and ShaKe history

Decoder Dictionary

Anthropological Mutation: One of the bases of our research. This concept explains how people got physically and mentally changed by technology.

BBS: Bulletin Board System. One of the cheapest, quickest and most democratic ways of trading information. There are about 130 000 on Earth.

Calusca City Lights: The most important political and countercultural bookshop in Italy. Founded in 1972 by Primo Moroni, myth-man of the underground and political extremism. It's now located inside *Cox 18* post-social centre because, as P. Moroni says: '*In the age of uncertainty it's right to work in a precarious place, one that may be cleared off tomorrow*'. In this bookshop many Decoder and ShaKe members shaped their identity.

Ladies and gentlemen, good morning. Today's program opens with... bzzz... bzzz... Decoder signifies decodifier...

We are like many Frankenstein's monsters, composed of human members and artificial elements created by technology. I've seen one whose hand had three fingers, with the thumb and index finger, substituted by a pair of pliers and functioning like a crooked beak. A small antennae came out of his mouth and he spoke in megahertz to a woman who had no ears, but instead two parabolic dishes to capture television messages. Not being able to comprehend each other, the two made love, in such a way that it excited my pity, now with clogged movement from the wheels on his feet, now facilitated by her tongue, magnetic-tape-made, sixty minutes long, while following the rythym of the electronic drum that beat in their chests. From this incest, DECODER was born, the child of communication, of diversity, and of provocation. It has no more mutations, like man it's completely technological. A small automaton, self-composed by many means of communication assembled anthropomorphically with the great hope of speaking a universal language. I hope that you can meet it and speak to it, if you can, wish yourself a good future, and I remind you that the transmissions are taken tomorrow morning, with DECODER it means...

With these words we opened the first number of

DECODER magazine in 1987. The group founders are formed of diverse cultural and political experience: anarchists, punks, communists, liberals and autonomists, all working in the field of communication - music, video, radio, graphics, literature, computers, photocopying and mail art. In reality, the project was born two years earlier from inside a bookstore in Milano.

Over there, the memory.

[nearly a scene from a science fiction novel]

At this point it's necessary to tell a little of the history of the situation of the *movement*, or what's called the underground scene in Italy. Here, whether you believe it or not, at the end of the seventies we were almost at the point of revolution. Illegal behaviour had taken a mass dimension and was diffused to an enormous level that was called the *counter-power*. Demonstrations, occupations of schools, self-reduction on ticket prices at concerts, expropriations - or massive theft at supermarkets, and violent attacks on the police, became everyday events. The authority had no degree of control over the situation, and the air that was breathed was very particular. Clearly, all of this influenced the behaviour and culture of thousands of youth. There was the sensation of having power and being able to change the course of history. Unfortunately, a series of armed groups mixed up *the sensation of having power* with the *flight of power*, and they radicalized the attack to prime a violent response from the state, which reacted by arresting 12,000 people in two years and proclaiming a special legislation, that was one of the hardest in the world. *Immediately* the air of freedom changed to an atmosphere of lead - making a black hole, a spacial and temporal gap, between the seventies and the growing eighties. The chaotic streets became deserted, post-atomic, where junkie zombies strolled, destined to die a short time after; they were the survivors of the atomic bombardment at the end of a dream. The party was over.

In this atmosphere of great suffering, a strange link was created with the past and its political action. There were

Decoder: Title of a 1984 movie by Klaus Maeck. In the movie F.M.Einheit, member of the band Einsturzende Neubauten, decodifies 'muzak', which is power structure music, and starts a revolution by spreading tapes of detourned music. From this movie we got inspiration for the name of our magazine. After all, how can you live in this age without a 'decoder'?

Encyclopaedia Psychedelica: English magazine published by Fraser Clark. His concept of 'zippy', the technological hippy, countercultural warrior of the new era, is simply fundamental.

Fetish: General theory unveiling the whole of human relations in our capitalistic society. Red line in Marxist research, it's also the base of our sexual preferences.

Galactic Party: Computer hackers meeting. Icata '89, which took place in Amsterdam, was of great importance for the first draft of a 'charter of human rights on information', which established that 'information wants to be free, uncontrolled and open to all'. 'Hacking at the End of the Universe', which took place in Amsterdam in 1993, was also of great importance.

Helter Skelter: Name of a self-run place inside Leoncavallo social centre, from 1984 to 1987. For experimental, radical and vanguardistic cultures only, it was the antithesis of pop culture. If you love the proletariat, you must give it complex culture. The most significant political action was the occupation, for three days, of a very famous theatre to stop a meeting of sociologists, psychoanalists, politicians about 'spectacular young gangs': that is, the young counterculture.

International (Situationist): Action and thought current of special importance for Italian countercultures. A form of total radical criticism leading to a revolutionary condition in continuous transformation.

Jones (Leroy): Afro-american poet, writer and essayist who changed his name to Amiri Baraka. He crossed 'beat', 'cultural nationalism' and marxist cultures. A man of great culture and dignity, a real revolutionary.

K: A magic letter. Some magic is necessary for our wishes to come true, especially if you are in a weak social category. That's why the fourth letter of ShaKe is capitalised.

Love: Countercultural fuel. Where love ends egoism and decline begin.

Milano: Our city. It's said that people out here only think about working. It was the cradle of the most radical movements, but now it's also nurturing the most dan-

people who tried at all costs to avoid the cultural force of the state to reconquer the ground floor, to cancel the human database and the memory of the years of the big dream, and who, on the contrary, were absolutely deprived of memory for generational reasons, they tried to open new streets of subversion. Like this, by a process of social genetics that could be defined as monstrous - the birth of a counterculture that saved the skin of many people: punk. In a monstrous manner, they copied the English experience, but with the originality of an incredible cultural and political collage. The devastating force of a few hundred kids had renewed a category of radical political action in Italy. In only five years, they counted tens of punk collectives, they occupied houses and abandoned factories, transforming them into workshops of communication to make music, punkzines, or just to stay together. This way of radical transformation of urban spaces with strong countercultural connotations was to be spread and called as 'the movement of the self managed social centres' ('movimento dei centri sociali autogestiti'). Between the absence of memory and no future, the punx created a temporal dimension, essentially that of the 'present'.

City Lights

In 1985, five young people who in diverse ways passed through the experiences mentioned above, met inside the bookstore *Calusca City Lights* in Milano. The bookstore was born in 1972, and modelled on the *City Lights* of San Francisco. For those who have not been to S.F., you could say that it's very similar to *Compendium* in London. Here in Milano, in the mid-'eighties, the battle between diverse conceptions of memory, which were argued over fiercely, was really hard - a situation in which diverse present experiences could not create interaction. At this point, the manager of the bookstore proposed to us the creation of a newsletter that would try to make transversal communication, and more profound relationships with all of the identities of the bookstore. The project failed, but our group of people, excited by the idea of creating human networks, decided to continue the research anyway, by founding a magazine and beginning to study a series of problems. The first objective layed down was the examination of linguistics, meaning, how to promote the principles of communication between different subjects. When we chose the temporal dimension in which to work we had no doubts: the 'future'.

On the starship

Many of our choices of that period were more spontaneous than reasoned, but we found ourselves exactly in the middle of an extremely confusing historic phase of changes throughout the world of production and phases of work. Whilst, in the cultural field, the crisis of punk opened new and large contradictions.

Living in chaos had become a normal condition, so we created a *DECODER* as an instrument for survival. That which we saw around us was a psychic dimension that we defined as an 'imaginative cloak' that prevented the sight of new utopias. This same concept was defined a few years later by Hakim Bey as the 'closure of the map'. Our *DECODER* had to search, projecting into the future, to create breaches in the block of the mind and to favour the birth of new imaginaries. The first area of study was that of the mutation of the body and of the spirit with respect to the epiphenomenon which heralded a new era: the invasion of technology. If we were able to demonstrate that transformations were already happening, the relation between peoples' temporal perceptions and the possibility of action in the present could be modified.

A view from outside: Cyberpunk!

For these reasons, we have always tried to bring articles about work together with forms of culture and the creative avant garde. The first numbers of *DECODER* included articles regarding production in outer space, how to revolutionize television, the demystification of the information sciences, on free festivals, Japan and drugs. These tendencies in the choices of themes have never been modified. At this point we started travelling throughout Europe and we discovered that there were other magazines, or groups, that had more or less our feelings and perceptions of

gerous organizations of the modern right wing (Lega Lombarda, Forza Italia). We kinda love it, but mostly would like it to burn.

No Copyright: Political-philosophical theory for the abolition of ownership rights over intellectual property. In the age of immaterial production and computer science it has become one of the most interesting fields for the creation of contradiction in capitalistic society.

Openness: Simply a way of life. It's about not being afraid of confrontation, about giving respect to what others think and being open to contamination. It's the base of multidimensional identity, of the movement against mental stillness.

Piazza Virtuale: Meaning 'virtual square', the most clever project we've seen on interactive TV. Run by the *Ponton Media Lab* from Hamburg, it allowed a revolutionary use of television, TV became a window on the world and an active tool of communication.

Questions: The aim of radical communication. The one who gives answers thinks in an ideological way, the one who creates questions is not looking for power and makes you think.

Revolution: We hope to see one soon... and not a

right-wing one.

Social Centres: Typically an Italian phenomenon ('centri sociali'). Aggregation centres self run by youngsters, mostly squatted places. After the big repression of political movements in the seventies, squats have been the only available places for political, cultural and self identity projects. Without them the eighties would have been even more terrible.

TAZ: Temporary Autonomous Zone. A fascinating political category created by Hakim Bey. It is like an uprising which does not engage directly with the State, a guerrilla operation which liberates an area (of land, of time, of imagination) and then dissolves itself to reform elsewhere/elsewhen, before the State can crush it. It looks like a good solution for the nineties.

Universe: the only battlefield of the 21st century. In our more and more localised world, the only likely solution is to become increasingly nomadic.

Vague: London magazine that kept its roots in punk culture and modernized itself at the same time. Tom Vague is some kind of Ballardian hooligan with a political-poetical spirit. He thinks globally and acts locally (in Portobello Rd.)

Women: They have the psychical power to stir up great storms. They play an

reality. The *Encyclopaedia Psychedelica* and *Vague* were our points of reference in the U.K., while in Germany there was the Chaos Computer Club. In exactly the same period, word was beginning to be heard of a new current in Science Fiction writing: 'Cyberpunk'. This label exists as a reality of human behaviour and was more or less interpreted as having one's 'head in technology and feet in the street. It was used as a point of symbolic reference for a series of people around the world who thought that technology could be used in an alternative or transgressive manner. Cyberpunk, in fact, represents the rebel-figure of the new era.

The Shake cooperative

As we didn't feel alone anymore and we had found sisters and brothers all over the global village, we had not only intensified in strength but, together with others, we founded a publishing co-operative. We wanted to extend the effectiveness of the messages of the magazine. This resulted in a series of books, videocassettes, multimedia installations and anything resembling a way of conceptualizing communication involving the libertarian culture, punk and cyberpunk. Our first book was titled *The Cyberpunk Anthology*. It was not a 'literary' anthology, instead it was put together with texts from real cyberpunk subjects: computer hackers, experimental artists, phone phreaks, enthusiasts and anarchists of technology. This book produced diverse reactions. It was a best seller (eleven editions were printed), many reviews were written in the press, and clearly it grabbed the eyes of the police (our office has been searched, and we we're the objects of two *relations* with the secret services). But most importantly, an enormous debate on the subject of freedom of information was unleashed. Now, when any Italian newspaper speaks of new information technology it is compelled to quote the alternative experience described in our book.

The hard work phase.

We understood at that moment that with a a lot of work we could change things. This is how we began to construct a catalogue of books that would be a kind of hammer for the heads of the people. Working 12-14 hours a day for four years we have been able to:

1) produce nine issues of *DECODER*, increasingly more of a magazine of social informatics and at the same time a publication for mutants. *DECODER* has around 50 contributors spread all over the world.

2) publish 15 books - and we have plans of publishing at least eight a year starting in 1994.

3) open a Bulletin Board System, that works like an everyday telematic journal for 400 users in the Milano area and an information network that has 23 hosts throughout Italy with around 2000 users.

4) organize about 30 media parties, where interactive installations are made and elementary courses for the use of new technology are given.

5) participate in over 250 debates on the questions of new technology and liberty of information.

It's clear that in all this process the philosophy of the 'refusal of work' has become a distant memory but, although in Italy state benefits or the dole don't exist, no one in ShaKe is paid for the work that's done. So, the relation with the market is peculiar.

Our intentions for the future are to create, through editorial activity, the conditions and the countercultural humus for the movement to regenerate. This is how it happened at the end of the sixties. We want to intervene into what could be called the 'crisis of the social center', a valid model of resistance during the eighties, but one that must necessarily mutate and evolve as we move toward the year 2000. In a paradoxical epoch, where the maximum diffusion of technology for the distribution of information corresponds with a minimum of real communication between social subjects, the only perspective is to reason around a hypothesis for upturning this relationship of domination.

important role in the ShaKe co-operative, in which they are the majority. Some of them created the *Chromosome X* group for the creation of a post-modern & post-genus theory of feminism.

X: The mathematical equivalent of unknown data. It stands for social uncertainty and embodies bourgeois fear of difference. Also used to provocatively hide one's bourgeois self identity and show a revolutionary one.

Yipl: Youth International Party Line. A magazine created in 1971 by Abbie Hoffman. It was the bulletin of yippies, dedicated to collecting and spreading hacking techniques, mainly against public phones.

Zerberus: Pattern and software of a telematic network invented by Hamburg's Chaos Computer Club. The underlying philosophy is to make network communication totally horizontal. This net lives on more than 200 nodes in Germany.

Rules of the Game
ALL NEW GEN
saboteur of big daddy mainframe
gamegirl

>Welcome to the world of ALL NEW GEN.

>Thank you for playing.

>In this game you become a component of the matrix, joining ALL NEW GEN in her quest to sabotage the databanks of Big Daddy Mainframe.

>You will use any means necessary to infiltrate and corrupt the controlling forces of Big Daddy.

>All battles take place in the Contested Zone, a terrain of propaganda, subversion and transgression.

>Your guides through the contested zone are the renegade DNA Sluts, abdicators from the oppressive superhero regime, who have joined ALL NEW GEN in her fight for data liberation.

>The path of infiltration is treacherous and you will encounter many obstacles. The most wicked - Circuit Boy - a dangerous technobimbo, whose direct mindnet to Big Daddy renders him almost invincible.

>You may not encounter ALL NEW GEN as she has many guises. But do not fear, she is always in the matrix, an omnipresent intelligence, an anarcho-cyber-terrorist acting as a virus of the new world disorder.

>You will be fuelled by G-slime. Please monitor your levels.
Bonding with the DNA Sluts will replenish your supplies.

>Be prepared to question your gendered biological construction.

>There will be opportunities throughout the game for pleasurable distraction.

>Be aware that there is no moral code in the Zone.

>Enjoy.

>In the spaces between words she searches for clues. >Pathways into the cyphered heart of Big Daddy. >The virus of the new world disorder takes on the transglobal fathernet of power and ambition. >Dirty work. For slimy girls. >Replicating her way through the Shadow's dingily seductive maze of data massage parlours, Freezers and Hots, Gen was inevitably reminded of Circuit Boy, aka Mission Improbable. Boy was rapidly losing his promise as an easy route into Big Daddy. Maybe he *was* just a mindless technobimbo, a limbless hole, good for a quick buttfuck or alpha exchange and not much else, as the Cortex Crones had predicted. Well, she'd suck on his memory some more, hardwire his balls and then see what else the Zone could offer. >Suck, fuck and split, as the Sisters say. >Any mission has its highs and lows, but this particular quest had been stranded on a barren plateau of spaghettied code and deviant data for too long. Dry and chaotic when she needed wet and elegant. >Big Daddy was becoming more ethereal with each transaction (the mythology expanding exponentially). His constructs were more ambiguous, more resistant to the mercenaries of slime. >She considered that an impasse is merely a state of mind and that with a subtle cognitive shift she could locate more yielding data. A shift is as a good as a holiday and she was overdue for some bonding with her sisters in slime, the lusciously wet DNA Sluts. >Although it had been a few weeks since she had bonded with the Sisters, Gen knew how to find them. She calculated... it was after midnight... they were true children of the Zone... one perfect environment... the Alpha Bar. >The Alpha Bar. The place for transgressive time out in the Zone. Provocative. Pornographic. Perverse. Her kind of place. Her kind of constructs. Every child player wins a prize. >Leaving the Shadow, Gen self-replicated through the Zone's biomembraned back blocks and reached the Alpha Bar in record time. As she'd determined, her Home Girls were well represented at the bar. >Beg, Bitch and Snatch were in a dark place, superbonding with some exotic tribal constructs. The feathers were flying. >Cunt was giving a couple of the Zone Boys a hard time about something, probably Smarts. She never could say no to drugs and rough Zone traders had their own perverse appeal for Cunt. >The Princess of Slime was visible by her absence. She was probably grinding her way through her favourite bar, The Space with No Face, followed as always by her acolytes, Fallen and Abject. >Sublime was blissing out on Dance, bonding to the rhythm, sliming to the beat. >As for the other Sisters, where they were and what they were doing was anyone's calculation. >Recreational options in the Zone were plentiful and diverse; Sex, Trance and Dance the most favoured. >Sliding through the press of bodies, constructs and grams, Gen selected one of her favourite bonding booths, placed her hand on the palm code reader and entered. It was a booth japonais, fitted out with futon, screens, antique pillow book, incense. As she had a rep for being the hottest bioconstruct on the block, the strangest attractor, she never had to wait long to replenish her slime banks. >She had transmutated into an Hispanic model of human female, optimised for the slime exchange. Gen pleasured herself, familiarising her sensors with the cool olive languidness of the body she had chosen. >A screen by the door displayed the image of a visitor. Mistress Beg. Requesting entry. >The door opened. Silk ropes in hand, the Mistress of Detestable Pleasure appoached Gen. Beg's method of bonding was dangerous, addictive and severe. Activated by stored memories, Gen's slime levels began a

Sex, Trance & Dance

slow rise. >The screen flickered on again. A geisha construct with a tray of sake and sashimi. She entered. Placed a redly laqueured tray on the low table. Served the sake. Waited. Beg instructed the geisha to return later, when her help would be required. Cruel anticipation. Gen's slime bank shivered to another level as the geishacon scrolled out.

The Contested Zone
BM
Circuit
Boy
A dangerous
echnobimbo
Big
Daddy
Mainframe
A transplanetary military-industrial-imperial
data-environment
BM

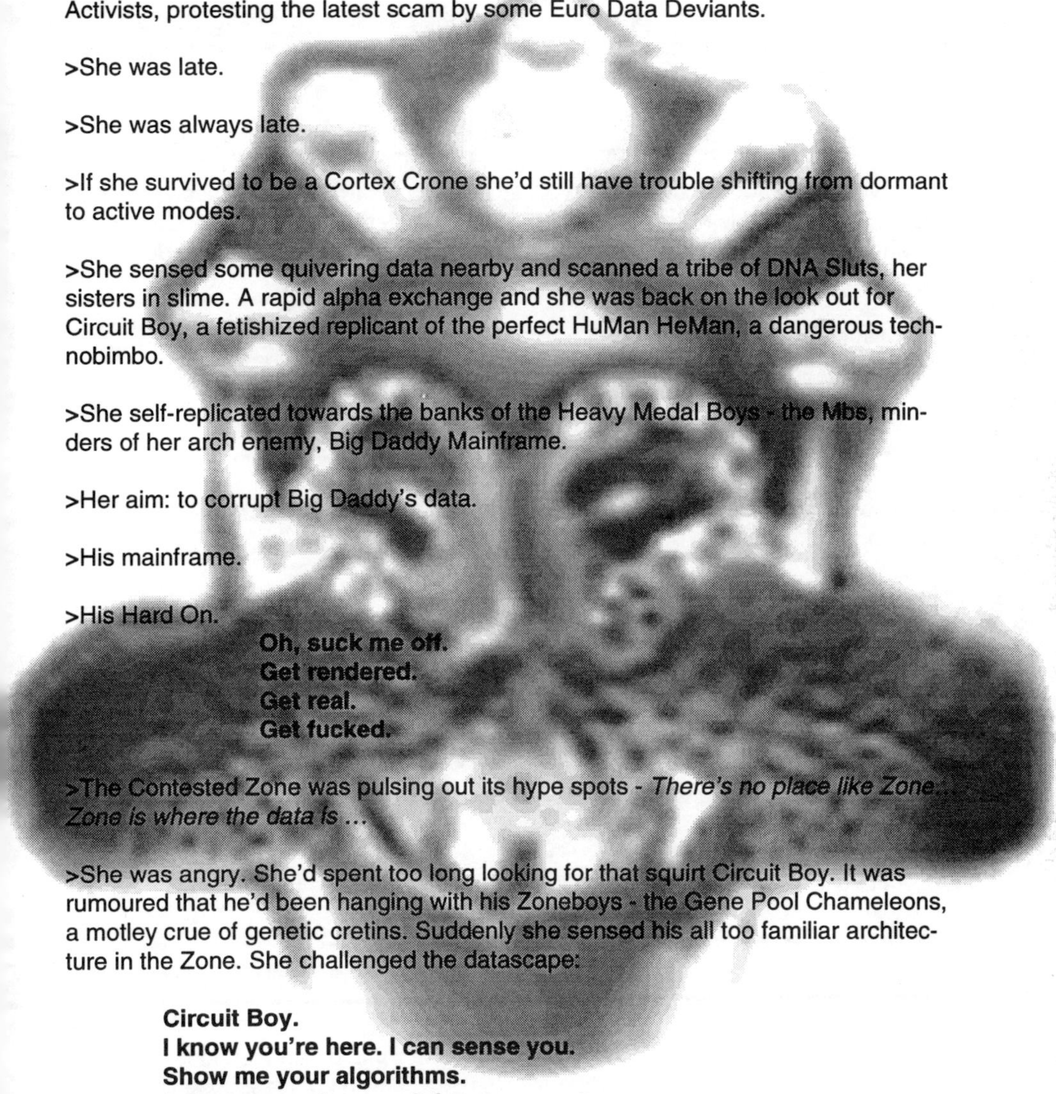

>A long wintered night in the Contested Zone.

>Gen's biological membrane shivered as she multiplied through a posse of Virtual Activists, protesting the latest scam by some Euro Data Deviants.

>She was late.

>She was always late.

>If she survived to be a Cortex Crone she'd still have trouble shifting from dormant to active modes.

>She sensed some quivering data nearby and scanned a tribe of DNA Sluts, her sisters in slime. A rapid alpha exchange and she was back on the look out for Circuit Boy, a fetishized replicant of the perfect HuMan HeMan, a dangerous technobimbo.

>She self-replicated towards the banks of the Heavy Medal Boys - the Mbs, minders of her arch enemy, Big Daddy Mainframe.

>Her aim: to corrupt Big Daddy's data.

>His mainframe.

>His Hard On.

Oh, suck me off.
Get rendered.
Get real.
Get fucked.

>The Contested Zone was pulsing out its hype spots - *There's no place like Zone... Zone is where the data is ...*

>She was angry. She'd spent too long looking for that squirt Circuit Boy. It was rumoured that he'd been hanging with his Zoneboys - the Gene Pool Chameleons, a motley crue of genetic cretins. Suddenly she sensed his all too familiar architecture in the Zone. She challenged the datascape:

Circuit Boy.
I know you're here. I can sense you.
Show me your algorithms.
Let me corrode your defenses.
Circuit Boy. Come here.
Let me buttfuck your irresistable chrome-plated ass, honey.
I want you.
Circuit Boy.
I'm waiting.

>In the domains of the abstract, Circuit Boy was an easy seduction.

>Boy had been designed for pleasure. He was the penultimate pleasure model, made for merging. Hard and abundant. Pleasingly shy. Full of holes and protuberances.

>Cunt draped a spline around his chrome rendered torso, talked dirty equations, algorithmically slid up and down on his double density, read only his memory (which was full of adolescent yearnings). She, slime incarnate, relentlessly manipulated and extended his many parameters. Artfully, together, they postponed the moment of full G-slime transference, rerouting urgent visceral requests to deeper levels of their source codes.

>The Mistress of Detestable Pleasure draped a spline around his wire frame.

>Her archives of pain and desire were immense.

>She rendered him senseless with her infinite promise of corruption.

>He allowed himself to be dragged outside the moral code, all precepts ignored, forgotten.

>He was zero to her triple cunt intelligence.

>Their boundaries merged, forming new objects.

>She mapped his changing parameters, calculating the pleasure options.

>She was abject-oriented desire to his open subject.

>It was in this way that Circuit Boy learnt the rewards of willing submission.

>Abject feigned sleep, her thighs slightly apart, her left breast uncovered.

>She favoured a non-linear approach.

>Her pathways were subtle.

>Circuit Boy tended her biological components, practising ethereal modes of convergence in his down time. He partitioned his RAM, slowing his response times to match her requirements. She was highly encrypted, he became expert at decoding.

>Their surveillence narratives grew so dense it was impossible to know who was in control.

The User

>I am the user

her visceral invocations/incantations annihilate my self in a glorious tirade, a torrent of organs and muscles and veins and skin. she separates my precious flesh

from my bones. she examines it with detachment but does not cast it aside. she makes contact, inserts her biology through the surface tension of my skin and plunges deep into the seething bile. she strips away the final vestiges of my constructed body and picks clean the bones. she wraps her insidious words around my feverish brain with her thousand arms. she is gentle and violent. with her perfect peripherals she dislodges my databank from the occiputal cavity and down loads digital propaganda direct from her fibre optic nerve centre. she corrupts me.
she scorns my debility. pronounces me weak she laughs at my desire to collapse into familiar flesh. her blasphemy is cleansing and transcendent. she the high priestess, the mistress of disgust, takes my heart, punctures the sentimental aorta, whispers her lovehorror into the drained chambers. she speaks in flaming tongues that i sometimes understand. she presents me simultaneously with no alternatives and many alternatives. she tells me my only hope lies beyond the coded skeleton. she offers me no clues and no comfort. she is uncompromising in her demands. i must form a body of difference. i have no maps. i am undone. i do not know myself. the future is bleak. i am afraid but

>I A M I N F E C T ED B Y H E R

Just say no.

©Henry Lydiate 1989
All rights reserved.
No part of this work may be reproduced or transmitted in any form or by any means, or stored in a retrieval system of any nature, without the written permission of the copyright holder.
No part of this work may be modified without the written permission of the author.
No part of this work may be exposed to public view in any form or by any means, without identifying the creator as author.

(No copyright claims will be made against publishers of non-profit editions.)

Anti-copyright, 1985, 1991. May be freely pirated & quoted—the author & publisher, however, would like to be informed at:

Not copyrighted. Any of the material in this book may be freely reproduced, translated or adapted, even without mentioning the source.

© You shouldn't need reminding, but remember, somebody holds the copyright on everything in here: specifically Deltamere Ltd and our contributors. Be cool. Use your head: if you're photocopying a few zines we won't mind. If you rip off copyright material for commercial gain, we will.

This pamphlet is anti-copyright and can be freely reproduced by any revolutionary group. But copyright protects it from being used by journalists, rich bastards, etc.

Contents are public-domain material reproduced from vintage newspaper publication and are not licensed nor authorized by the original copyright or trademark owners.

All rights reserved. No part of this book may be reproduced or transmitted in any form or by any means without the express written consent and permission of the publisher.

Copyright and reproduction: Non-profit community groups have permission to reproduce parts of Streetwize Comics, as long as the original meaning is retained and proper credit is given to Streetwize Comics.

© Copyright

NOT TO BE COPIED IN ANY SHAPE OR FORM WITHOUT THE ARTISTS PERMISSION

A copyright free publication.

© Christopher Gray, 1974. Normal copyright is held on this book. Anyone, however, who wishes to reproduce material contained within it **on a non-profit-making basis** is free to do so, in whole or in part, in any way they see fit.

CONCERNING THE FOLLOWING "COPY PAGES": Although this idea is highly abnormal for a commercial book, you are invited to photocopy these pages yourself (or even hit a quick-print shop and have hundreds made) AND THEN **SPREAD THEM THROUGHOUT YOUR WORLD AS YOU SEE FIT.** REPRODUCE ONLY THE PAGES HEADED "COPY PAGE". DO NOT REPRINT ANYTHING ELSE FROM THIS BOOK WITHOUT PERMISSION OF THE PUBLISHER.

Copyright SCAT. Any part of this pamphlet may be reproduced freely by tenants groups, community groups and trade union organisations.

Aporia Press, 1987. No copyright: please copy & distribute freely.

Pages may be photocopied for classroom use, with an acknowledgement to ©.

JUST SAY N©

This is not the alarm clock that woke Ronald Maynard for work every morning from 1966-1979. RIGHT: Software tool box for retouching photographs.

Above the bathroom mirror
reads a note
Ronald Maynard in Egypt 1944
This is not the image you have of yourself
FOOTNOTE
National Dog of Great Britain, 1945: "I've a hearty grip for a friend and a hearty grip for a foe and he that would put England down has a mighty rough road to go."

Images aren't **static** even when still. They **reflect**, like a well arranged mirror, the things we want to **see.** Half of the image never **appearing**, **trap**ped inside **the** motivations for **making** it or for **seeing** it. **Cities,** states and individuals represent themselves by their faded images: uncomfortable memories, half forgotten in the guilt of a subjectively

Justified **Propaganda**

PUT THE PIECES IN THEIR PLACE: A Nazi jigsaw produced during the Second World War. It attempts to suggest Jewish influence in the British media.

RIGHT: Great granddaughter of Ronald Maynard remembering him through stories told around photographs.

Images are better than memories **memories,** opportunities to "shared experience." Today's image: tomorrow's two-dimensional focus for **memory,** or its replacement.

The Cenotaph, Whitehall. London by night: On the reverse of this post card from 1928 is written *"This is a real photograph. All being well, Peggy and Charlie will come over tomorrow."*

A HAPPY BIRTHDAY
UNCLE

London replicates itself:
postcards of past **Victor**ies
activating present complicity.
Birthday, Xmas, journeys
and those special events. Images of where we are,
sent to those left behind. A paper trail laid in time. Just in
case we ever get ....lost.

Safe in my armchair, feet up and resting my head on a pillow formed from complicity, I switch the remote. Pictures flicker and die, trapped in the shadows of motivation. They play the back of my retina and in turn play me. Like the tape makes technology sing. Sony, Mitsubishi, Philips, a small box I brought home acts as my emotional playground. Watch it with people to be on my own. Watch it on my own to be with people. Turn it off.

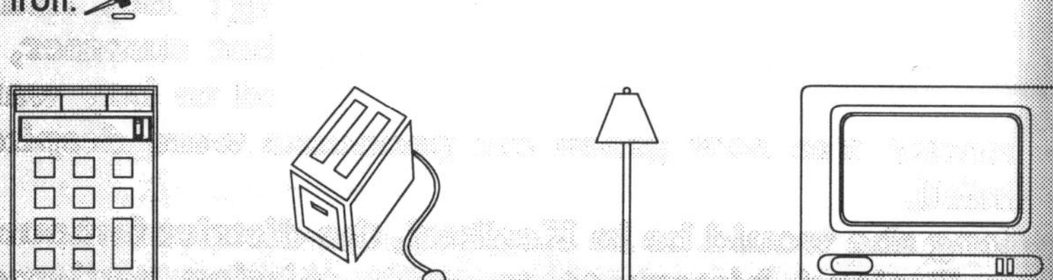

CHAIRMEN OF UNILEVER: F.J. Tempel. 1956-1966. H. S. A. Hartog 1966-1971. Lord Heyworth, 1941-1960. **BOTTOM RIGHT:** Product re-presented for *Underground*, 1993.

Reaching down.

What-**i**-want catalogues tease me with **appear**ances, somehow still **....connected....** to the **objects** from which they were **snap**ped... **Finger prints** that >>>**lead** to the **arrest of innocence.** Never satisfied, I put the **picture** on my wall. An **icon** of desire. **Lawn-mowers, car-radios** and **promises of sex.** Reality reads better when seen between two sheets of paper, trapped in the endless **reassurance** of ever **larger print runs.** Replicate it. Make it true. Replicate it. Make it true.

Replicate it. Make it true.

Replicate it. Make it true.

So much time **£ (spent) £** on maintaining fantasies for others to bathe in **(self)**deception, always.... for others. An **addict**ion formed, to be paid back **weekly**, or if you prefer, sign up for six months and get one ***free......*** **Money talks**: and has nothing to **say.** After all, how many **washing machines** can you really use? Stimulate me to **£(acquire.)£** Why don't you? Gratified, I'm **anaesthetised** against injustice once again.

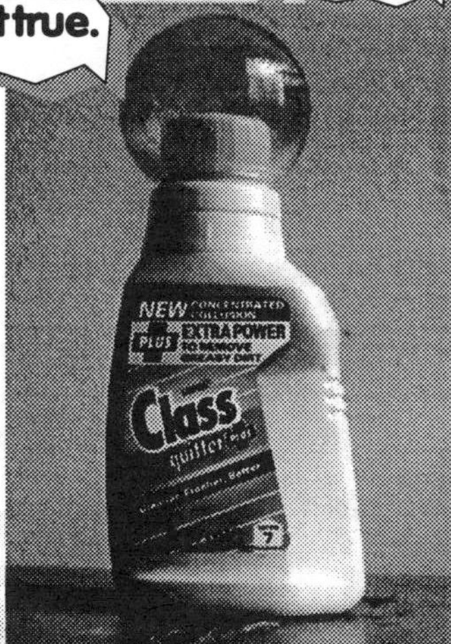

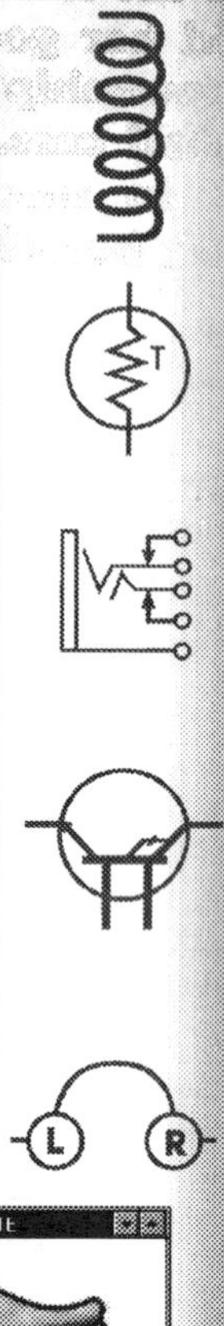

"See me getting on this plane? You know, we couldn't afford real holidays then... So we pretended..."

FOOTNOTE

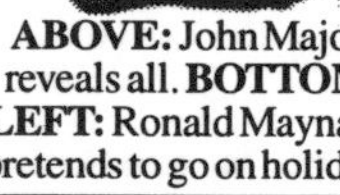

ABOVE: John Major reveals all. **BOTTOM LEFT:** Ronald Maynard pretends to go on holiday.

Subjective, this photo portrait acts as your **yard stick,** against which you **measure me.** Carefully charting, the signs of ageing. Give up the responsibility of memory. Hand it over the counter. Pay the **cost...** £4.50 at **Boots, Happy** Snapper, or **Kodak.** We can all carry around the **24** hour ***footnotes*** to experience, developing the evidence of what happened, for some future **court-room** or **interrogation** arranged by friends.

"Is that your boy?" "Do you see him much." "Not since the car crash."

Family snaps, life-jackets of love. The empty husks of holidays from horror. Now turned to portholes of hurt through which the tears flow. Sinking the ship but releasing the crew.

Set the self timer for physical admissible evidence.

FOOTNOTE

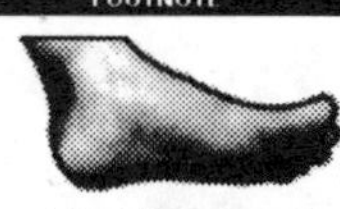

ABOVE: Ronald Maynard poses for family snap. **LEFT:** Camera ad.

I defy myself by image, whether bought, or acquired through behavioural problems. If I feel low, I **buy** myself a little something. **Add**ing to myself like a little insect, eating its victims and strapping the corpses on its back, attempts to ward off predators. Looking in shop windows I'm reflected, mounted for sale, in what will get me on at the office or the party. The mirrors in the high street convince me that this image or that will allow entry to forbidden places. You pay for quality, a sharpness of image. To get things in focus. **Captured** appearance chains itself to the original **object,** like a finger print leads to the arrest of the suspect.

PAUSE

Part 2
Lies
after telling the truth
MADE IN ENGLAND
MADE IN ENGLAND
5A
5A
5A
5A

Science Fictions (5 Perspectives)

1. The fossilised light that is photography has often been ascribed a special GLUE, between itself as a fugitive REALITY and the permanency of material things. The usual description has photography as the FINGERprint of a physical REALITY, captured within a process legally quantified by the RITUAL processes of scientific positivism.

2.(A) With at least 10% of all images appearing in US magazines and periodicals digitally altered, image (RE)-processing is mortally wounding the incontestable in the field of seeing.

2.(B) Photography in its hey-day represented a chemically fixed way of seeing, taken from a single PERSPECTIVE from which the witness (a photographer) records EVENTS.

3. Photography has maintained a central platform in the RITES of possession in what will surely be remembered as the positiv(IST) modern(IST) (ISM) century, a time of rigid ritual monoliths of ideology fabricated and ENacted for the consumption of useless commodities, made out of the (UN)justified rape of (RE)sources that are morally maintained by images of PROGRESS.

4. The POSITIVism of fixed perspectives has FAILed to live up to the HYPE of a trajectory toward the utopic. It dies in a public withering, QUESTIONed in law and banished from existence by the forensic SCIENCE imPRISONed within cases like those of the Guildford 4 or Birmingham 6.

5. We sit at the end of the twentieth century, WITNESSes to the (re)-invention of religion, a REFORM-ation of the subjectivity of social control a TELEcommunications construction of TRUTH? New forms of technology replicate demonic communion, WHIPPing up a fervour of powerful VISIONS that seduce us into digesting them.

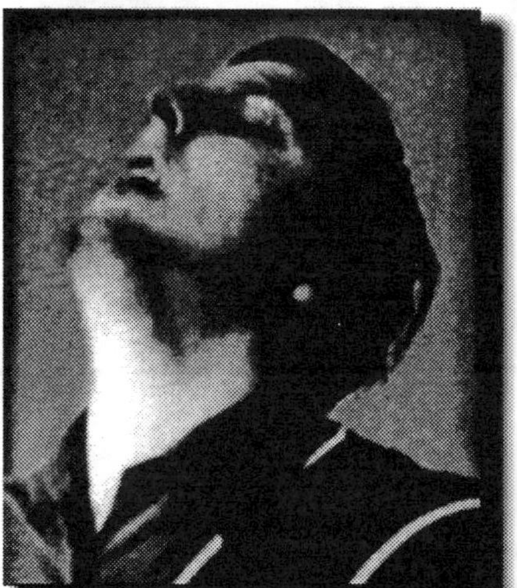

Let him have it

The Witness

On the 2 November 1952 Chris CRAIG and Derek BENTLEY broke into a London warehouse. BENTLEY had a KNIFE, CRAIG a REVOLVER. The two youths were seen entering the premises and the POLICE were called. A detective climbed on to the roof. CRAIG shouted defiance at him, but BENTLEY surrendered. At this point, BENTLEY is alleged to have shouted, "Let him have it, Chris." CRAIG fired, and the bullet grazed the officer's shoulder. CRAIG blasted at the police reinforcements. The first policeman to appear in the rooftop doorway was shot in the head. Craig then ran to the edge of the roof and jumped off. He landed 30 feet below, fracturing his spine and left wrist. It was clear from the start that the 16-year-old was too young to be hanged, even though he had fired the fatal shot. At Bentley's trial, much depended on the jury's interpretation of his rooftop shout to CRAIG, which apparently incited him to murder. In the witness-box, CRAIG admitted his hatred for the police, although he denied intending to kill PC MILES. BENTLEY, a "working class illiterate and educationally subnormal," was ill equipped to answer questions satisfactorily. The jury took 75 minutes to find the two youths guilty of murder. CRAIG was sentenced to be detained at Her Majesty's Pleasure. BENTLEY was sentenced to death. Various appeals from his family and the public failed to win a reprieve, and he was HANGED on 28 January 1953.

FOOTNOTE

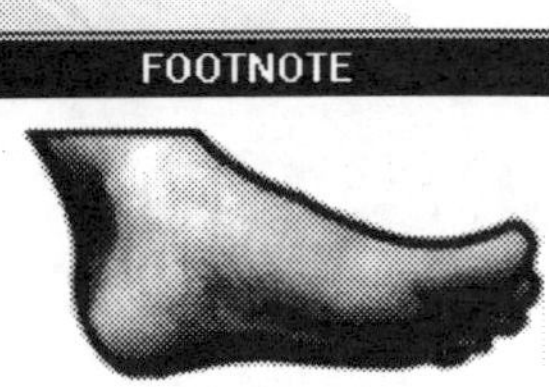

TOP: Craig's knuckleduster, lent to Bentley.
RIGHT: Bentley goes back to prison.
Since the death of Bentley, psychic phenomena have been reported, the family Vicar speaking in the voice of Derek.

BELIEF in what some one says allows us to construct a "TRUTHFUL" and "BELIEVABLE" "PICTURE" of the world, allowing us to navigate the MENTAL spaces that lie between people. The immediate testimony given in the injustice courts acts as a witness to action. It is often only by bringing the character of the witness

into question that a case is disproved. Testimony is seen as BELIEVABLE subjectivity because the witness, character references hold good. DEREK BENTLEY, an "educationally subnormal working class illiterate" had no quality references. Our belief in photography as direct attestation is similar. As long as we believe in the chemical processes that hold an image in place, we are able to construct "TRUTHFUL" and "reliable" models of the domain in which we operate. In a world constructed as much by symbolic action as physical behaviour, image production acts as the artifactual evidence of the bond between mental and physical geographies. For most image production and consumption is a matter of ritual, a symbolic ordering of memory.

RENTAL
£2.00
per night

STEREO
ON LINEAR TRACKS

15

FOOTNOTE

In recent times the Bentley case has been retold in the film *Let him have it* directed by Peter Medak, screenplay by Neal Purvis and Robert Wade.

CONTINUATION:
Iris Bentley continues to fight for her brother's pardon.

"The hanging… one of the most jolting scenes in British cinema." THE INDEPENDENT

By these imaging RITES, individuals bind into the collective life of families, groups and societies of SELF INTEREST. If such ritual ordering is successful, the participants feel connected, both with themselves and with society. The bodies of mental and physical GEOGRAPHERS locate and fuse together to form strong FICTIONS of a given time and space.

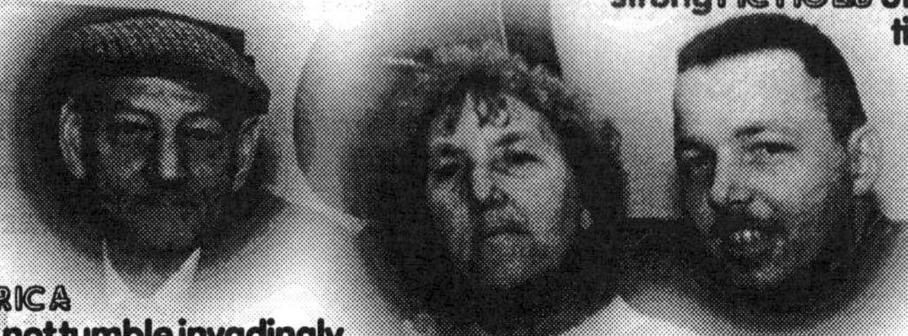

AMERICA
need not tumble invadingly
into the physical space of bedrooms.
Telecommunications empires have preceded it by years (don't sell me America SELL me Hollywood). Posters stuck to the back of my door, caught up in cyclic collisions of news of the newsworthy making the news. Public events become important by their very recording. The "TRUTH", strongly fictional in every detail, becomes direct testimony taking place all around us: logged, catalogued and preserved in the basement of BBC's references of importance. Events ritually tamed in this way become the captives of their own appearance, neatly ordered to situate me somewhere between Madonna, Mother Theresa, and Death Poverty and his All-Stars.

Photography stands, then, as the most "natural" way of referring to appearances, a dominatrix of the mental spaces established between people, a point of view built to the beat of drums, Hitler Youth, or the matching Yarrow feet up Oxford Street (and then those same feet marching back down Oxford Street because, apparently, the cameras weren't loaded.) Some way back, deep in the age of black and white cinema between the casualty blankets of 1914 and 1939, words slid from view and into disrepute, as the most "NATURAL" way of relating immediate testimony. The 1930s saw advertising become a crucial economic force - the cement of the "NEW DEAL" of cinema. We became addicted to images as a natural way SEEING.
Photography is sanctioned TRUTH, blessed by quantifiable science and maintained in the CHEMISTRY of silver. This procss has a covenant with IRELAND, AUSCHWITZ, BHOPAL and HIROSHIMA, despotic achievements of the twentieth century. This process exhibited a RITUAL power beyond the enjoyment of other image-systems. Unlike its ancestors, it was not dependent on the individual IMAGE maker. The photographer intervenes in setting up and guiding the image making PROCESS, but the ritual itself remains an optical-CHEMICAL one: a pure, positivist exhalation.

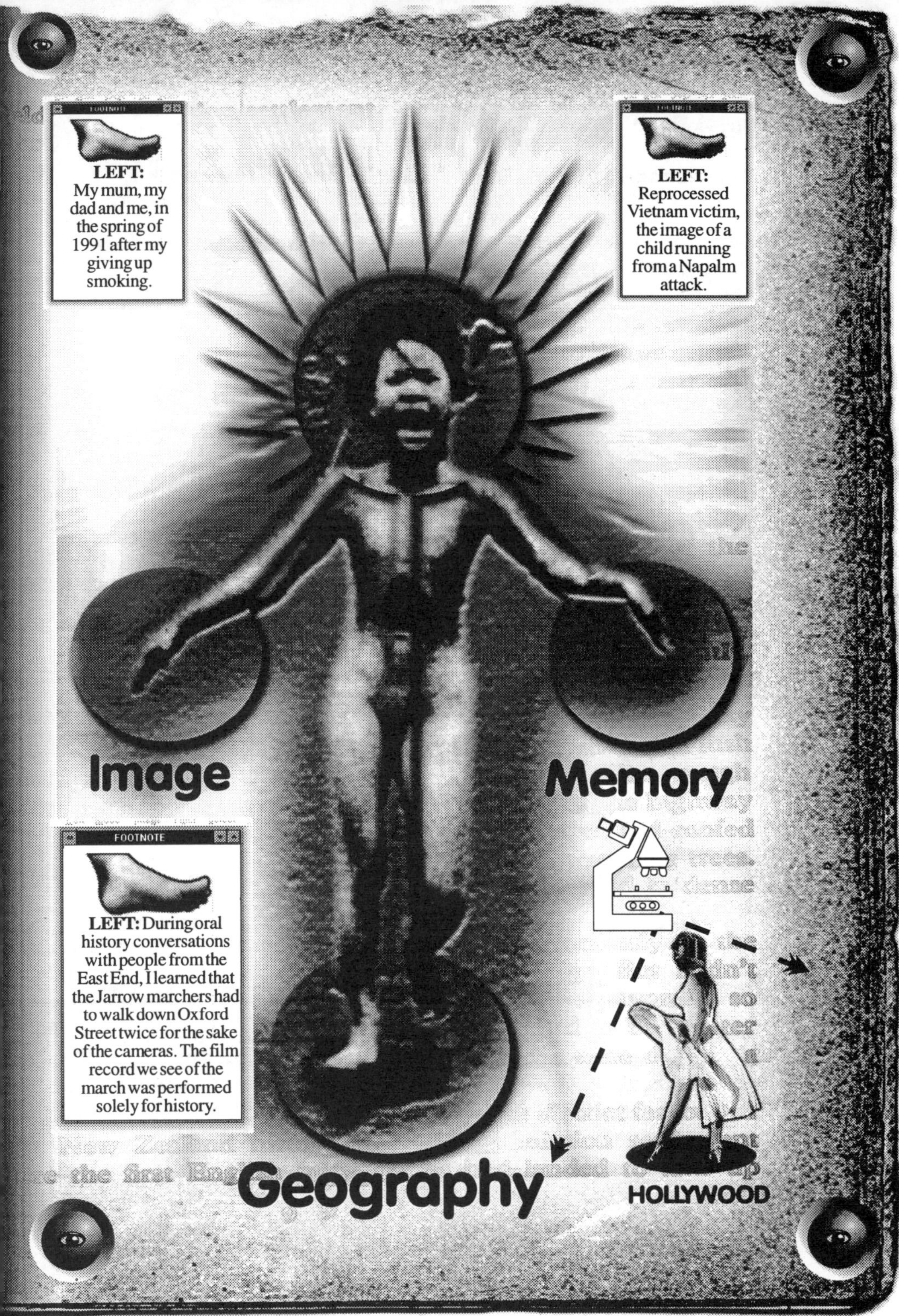
FOOTNOTE
LEFT: My mum, my dad and me, in the spring of 1991 after my giving up smoking.
FOOTNOTE
LEFT: Reprocessed Vietnam victim, the image of a child running from a Napalm attack.
Image
Memory
FOOTNOTE
LEFT: During oral history conversations with people from the East End, I learned that the Jarrow marchers had to walk down Oxford Street twice for the sake of the cameras. The film record we see of the march was performed solely for history.
Geography
HOLLYWOOD

First ReMove The Body:

Chemicals on paper and light refracted by precise lenses and the HABITual reliance on our eyes for our survival in the face of adversity, have created at best a complacent attitude toward the boringly-normalised and powerful-ordinariness of public (ab)USES of photography. This habitual reliance has left us ILL - equipped and fearfully IGNORANT of the development of powerful digital process. Computers can now synthesise the familiar "truth-to-APPEARANCE" aesthetic that was photography, ACTing as a similar skin over a very different cultural body. Digital cloning has KILLED the "original genius" making the plagiarist king in a land in which Anti Copyright becomes a lifestyle option. Alongside the entanglements of authorship created by technological advance, lie the shattered windows of visual truth from which we emerge, bloodied but still intact.

Now SewOn The Skin:

Digital technologies create a photography that is not photography, linking us to geographies of illusion without the need to reference a "real." This process (RE)invents HIStory, pointing toward a truth that is the strong fiction of HIStory. Excluded, our physical and mental bodies invite an irreversible AMNESIA in which everything continues to function the same. Events seem to take place and can eventually seem to amount to a HIStory. Then, surreptitiously, we no longer know what is, and what is not, or are even in a position to decide.

Sew on the skin of the dead donkey of history. Parade it in the street. Welcome this passing, for this is the history of forgetting, celebrate three reasons for festival.

THE END: Of epic images of Victories sailing up the Thames safely guarded by a collective loss of memory.
THE END: Of the ship's crew conveniently out of sight. No more extras for the film set; stolen men, lying beaten, ripped and raped from families.
THE END: Of foreign beggars to the history of amnesia, emerging from the fearful warrens of (self)protection.
This was the twentieth century, a convenient lapse of memory of abusing male toxic logic, pricks pointing to women, saluting images of others flesh sacrificed on the way to Hollywood's vast glamour of swashbuckling adventure. These are the waste products of living with ghosts, the invisibles, the knowing who has to pay and who can't afford it.

Images you have seen before but you cannot remember when.

1

I have never seen a black mugger but can never remember a time when I did not know what he looked like.

2

I have never seen a bender fuck a child but can never remember a time when I did not know what it looked like.

FOOTNOTE

In centuries past, British naval successes were celebrated by processions, including the *Victory*, sailing up to Thames to Greenwich. The ships' crews were always hidden from public view.

3

I have never seen the Statue of Liberty but can never remember a time when I did not know what it looked like.

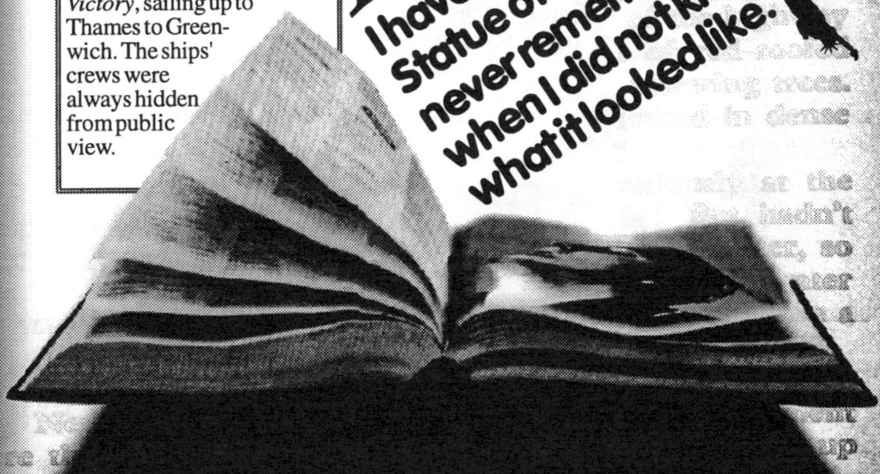

Harness the Trojan Horse

Digital imaging is being taken up in silence behind people's backs by such divergent activities as civil engineering, war reporting, military reconaissance, PORNOgraphy, family albums, the business "community" etc. This is happening at speed and is surely an indication of its PROfound, central applicability to advanced capitalism or at least, it has UNleashed the cultural forces of an ULTRA-modernist society obsessed with the production of the RITUAL-imagery of possession.

But

Digital graphics can subvert strong FICTIONS of physical truth and, in so doing, make a challenge to the photograph's strict Aristotelian unities of time and place. The MENTAL geography that is the space between PREfabricated signs and immediate testimony is hung in part with the hoardings of those who can afford to advertise there. They surround us with the WEB of replicated transMISSIONS we bump into when we turn on the program or TUNE into to the FREQUENCY. And, into those areas where transmission is impossible, we are encouraged to carry the prefabricated signs of "MEANINGless consumables"; signs onto which we carefully graft our own sentiment; TROJAN horses stuffed with the CADAVERS of half-forgotten experience. As we become increasingly dissatisfied with a self-IMAGE mediated by redundant positivism in a century of WASTE-products, we can begin to take ADvantage of the broken windows of visual truth.

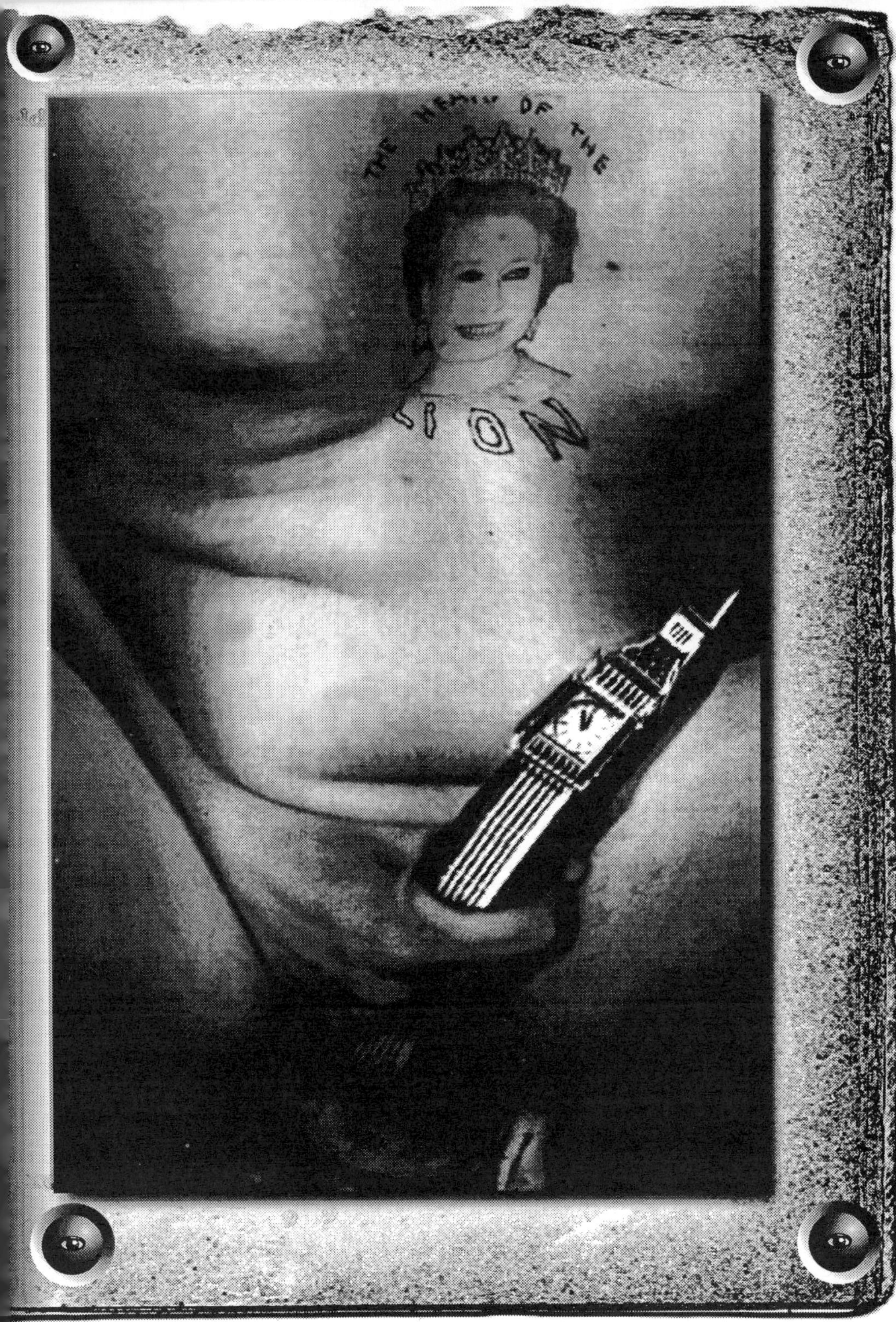
OF THE
LION

Tales of Pageant & Pantomime

A Technological Narrative for a Virtual Aristocracy

Richard Wright

Louis XIV, at the height of his glory, did not possess one hundredth of the power over nature and the ways to amuse oneself that are enjoyed today today by so many men of rather lowly status.
Paul Valery, 1928.

The Only Limit Is Your Imagination
W Industries promotion, (simulator and VR games manufacturer), 1991.

Even though dictators can't help turning excess into an art form, the Ceausescu residence is a world-class monument to cheap glamour and ersatz luxury. Just look at the swimming pool in this Everest of vulgarity - indoors (of course), but surrounded by fabulously complex mosaics and enough stained glass to furnish a medium-sized Gothic cathedral.
Loyd Grossman, 'Homes of the Dictators'.

There are many narratives at work to create our modern mythology of technology, yes, but the foremost is the utopian projection of a society of freedom, leisure and personal indulgence. Its commercial reflection takes the form of an unlimited orgy of consumption: an ability, part economic, part industrial, to gratify the 'desiring subject' to the extremes of satiation. Its promise is pursued in fact with the speed of the media to bring that which was out of reach, inaccessible due to geography or class, right up into the living room: onto the TV set, out of the hi-fi speakers, onto the table and inside the magazine. To help us better order our estate in relation to these proffered fineries, we are allowed to see our own appetites quenched through the lives of stars and celebrities who, by their example to us, glow with the talents they have developed for gracious living. And so an unrestrained appetite for consumption is personified by these few fortunates determined enough, or lucky enough or crooked enough to have achieved the means to lift that yearning from their shoulders.

Fancy champagne all the way as you indulge your wildest fantasies? Get your free Millionaires Club Gold card in next week's magazine and this could be you...
Advert for newspaper lottery, 'Sunday Express'.

The lives of those chosen few are held out to us as evidence of the existence of a pinnacle of power and luxury, ratifying the logic of social ambitions. But this small circle is handicapped by the same same social mobility that first granted its members the opportunity to rise above their fellows. Their ultimate position and status is always based (they must admit with shame and a curse on their forebears) upon a vulgar and lowly commercial dealing and financial success. Tainted by the sin of 'usury', they are marked out at Court and Church by a life tied to trade and moneylending. Their achievement is only the economic fortune of the merchant class, they can never aspire to the prestige of those who claim wealth as their birthright. Paul Getty fought to his dying breath to buy his way into the elite strata of high society, but he always remained just another lucky tycoon. Those whose blue-blooded destiny is to stand at the highest echelons - the nobility, the descendants of the crowned heads of Europe, the 'old' money of the landed gentry - still jealously guard their lineage from the soiling of interlopers. These thoroughbreds are those in whose veins flows the blood of the natural heirs of Adam, pledged to uphold the divine right of Kings and who, together, protect the mystique of monarchy.

And so the shipping tycoons, oil magnates and arms dealers compete with each other for the company of counts and princesses, all scrambling for proximity to the ultimate symbol of status that money just can't buy, which only the accident of birth or design of marriage can bestow, the final triumph of breeding and class over individual enterprise. This is the only true legitimation of wealth, acceptance by a cul-

ture that alone can furnish the proof that they have the personal worth to deserve their fortunes.

And, for an instant, she stared directly into those soft blue eyes and knew, with an instinctive mammalian certainty, that the exceedingly rich were no longer even remotely human.
William Gibson, 'Count Zero'.

For those excluded from wealth or status, the situation is less galling. For these souls the outer trappings of power should still be sufficient to motivate their labours. If the lottery or football pools fail to deliver, then they can look to media technology to provide a window onto the world of glamour and privilege, making images of luxury and decadence ready for domestic consumption. Or else, how about a day out to view the treasures ossifying in museums, palaces and stately homes, their reconstructions of period settings, decor and lifestyle all carefully roped off and restricted? Helping to construct a social dynamic of unnattainable aspirations, opulence and instant fulfilment, these institutions orient a social underclass towards the personal goals that will ensure their commitment to a life of unending striving and productivity.

The carpets of the palace were covered in gold decorations; silk paper hung on the walls and Persian carpets covered the floors. Bath taps, toothbrush holders and even toilet brushes were solid gold. Every inch of the palace realised the larger-than-life dreams of the small man who had always longed to a be giant.

But now the media circus of glamour, of lifestyles of the rich and famous, has gotten ahead of the game. Its orchestration of desire is now successful to the point that a part-time life of sublime affluence can now be partaken by proxy - distanced yet still present through gossip columns and reproduction antiques. Now, for those for whom the endless yearning for closer propinquity with the ruling classes is still not satiated, media technology can offer one last, one ultimate vehicle of social transportation.

Through vicarious experience and virtual environments the lives of ordinary people, the 'bungled and the botched', can be so immeasurably enriched when they are taken to elegant situations and suroundings far beyond the reach of their mundane lives and economic circumstances. In the present day, technology's promise of omnipotence is held to offer the individual a regal state of instant gratification. The limits of their desires are inscribed by the attainability of a lifestyle of supreme self-indulgence and privilege - modelled on the scale of the great age of Royalism and Absolute Monarchy.

The aristocratic aesthetic is the conclusion of a logic that runs from aspiration to affluence to leisure. The allure of monarchy is not only an economic site for the myth of limitless choice, but also a political and social one. The Monarch *deserves* to exercise his pleasures. This is the reward for his heritage of refined taste, superior cultural judgement and social status. And it is for our tourists of the digital powerscape to witness the fruits of such an edifying discrimination informed by perfect etiquette and leisured sensibilities.

To the ill-educated Ceausescu - he left school at 14 - valuable art works belonged together, whatever the style. So antique Greek statues stood in front of brightly coloured modern mirrors in a gaudy mixture of ancient and modern.

The fantasy of Virtual Reality grants the inferior classes the ability to take their leave within the framework of cyberspace, it domesticates the trappings of Kingship, but obliges the adoption of the manners of the class of superior sensibilities, perceptions, language and culture, of the class that owns this lifestyle. The culture of the lower class, unaccustomed to coping with the range of pleasures and fantasies now available, must be sacrificed - to be able to develop the social skills needed to pick and choose surroundings and recreations with delicacy and finesse. The technologies of the imagination shift the site of class opposition to a place where it can be resolved by the reward of an aristocratic aesthetic for centuries of patience and suffering. The only price is the neccesity for the common people to disown their class culture as obsolete. Aristocratic sensibilities are offered as the only alternative to more modest forms, the only psychological role model able to deal with extreme demands of technologically mediated subjectivity. Can the attainment of a state of intoxicating power be negotiated without aspiring to a culture of opulence?

The distance between social classes has traditionally been expressed by forms of mimicry, parody and satire. These provide the cultural tools whereby aristocratic manners are reconstructed under new terms of reference. The vogueing balls that blossomed in the early eighties, based in black and gay New York communities marginalised by Reagan's America, provided a way to come to terms with the social stereotypes to which they would not and could not conform. These strategies are as old as class itself - the lifestyles of pomp and circumstance are all parodied by genres such as carnival, *Mardi Gras* and pantomime.

Devoted film fans, (Ceaucescu) and his wife had their own velvet-lined cinema. At least once a week they held a screening of Scott Fitzgerald's 'The Great Gatsby'.

The Royal pageants of state occasions are strictly trafficked and off-limits. The 'traditions' of monarchy, most of them carefully designed by Prince Albert in

Victorian times, provide visible evidence of the political forces that are controlling behind the scenes. The pantomime is an inclusive communal event, the principal characters needing no birthright to legitimise their performance. They need only a layering of costume and make-up to contrive their appearance, and a repertoire of stage sets and acting rituals in order to take part .

Synthetic media substitute the substantialities of power for the simulation of its trappings. For the aspiring commercial classes, rich but untitled, this must become the final insult. Their position now doubly grave, spurned by the arbiters of taste they hoped to emulat, and having ostracised themselves from the vulgar habits and pastimes of their forebears, they still insist on the privilege of actuality, the tangibility, of the assets they have accumulated. They try to ignore the mockery of the virtual.

As robots and automatons replace living labour with dead labour, we confront the potential abolition of work itself, presenting us with a lifestyle of leisure and gentility. Technology creates a space in which it satirises the birthright of nobility by offering power over appearance and experience. Etiquette is a process of cultural exclusion, it puts a No Trespassing sign on the gate-posts of cultured leisure. Media technology allows a pantomime of manners to be orchestrated amongst the virtual reflections of aristocracy. Material possessions can be suppressed within the synthetic landscape and the conflicts of class identity can be played out. Social aspirations are turned into an ignoble performance where the working classes can test their unworthiness of the rewards of success and heritage.

New Orleans and Mardi Gras *are inextricably intertwined. The first European to set foot on this land, the French explorer Ibraville, makes camp on a swampy bayou thirty miles upriver from the mouth of the Mississippi. Tuesday March 3rd, 1699 -* Mardi Gras *day. Ibraville claims the land in the name of his king, Louis XIV, the town that springs up nearby is named for his cousin the Duc d'Orleans.*

In 1803, the French sign the Louisiana Purchase. New Orleans, now the property of the United States, for the first time a city without a king. Perhaps to compensate, today kings are commonplace, at societies' celebrations, and at the heads of parades. And during the two weeks of carnival sixty parades snake their way through the city.
"Farewell to the Flesh", American Chronicles, Lynch / Frost Productions.

THE SUN KING

Notes on contributors

Mandie Beuzeval uses image processing software and photography to investigate the mechanisms and devices of medicine. *"I see myself as an amateur detective stalking hospital environments gathering clues then arranging elements for the viewer to collect and find their own solution."* Write to her c/o Underground, PO Box 3285, London, SW2 3NN, UK.

Maxine Boobyer is an artist living and working in Cardiff and London. Developing her concerns with power relationships and the myth of architectural transparency, Maxine picks over an image of the modern counter window. The borders between communication and contamination are chewed up. The foreign body is absorbed, the mediation spat out. A new organising body begins to form. Contact Maxine c/o Underground, PO Box 3285, London, SW2 3NN, UK.

Decoder are a collective who, as described in their article, are primarily responsible for bringing cyber-punk sensibilities to cultural and social activism. They invite you to get in contact and to send material to them at: Shake Edizione, Via C. Balbo, 10 - 20136 Milano, Italy.
DECODER BBS: +39-2-29527597 (from 4 a.m. to 8 a.m.)
E-Mail: decoder@stinch0.csmtbo.mi.cnr.it

Fintan Friel: *"1935 seeks to indicate the presumptions and expectations that are relative to the context of propaganda. In this way it can help spark the recognition of a variety of ideological conditionings, and perhaps open the way to a challenge being offered. 1935 is advertising. 1935 is a caricature. 1935 is the past. 1935 is the future. You tell me."* Fintan Friel, Castlebar Road, Westport, County Mayo, Ireland.

Matthew Fuller is a genetically enhanced, chemically preserved, surgically improved editor of the paper *Underground* and a systems operator of the Fast Breeder bulletin board. He can be mailed c/o Underground, PO Box 3285, London, SW2 3NN, UK.

Graham Harwood is the author of *'If Comix - Mental'*, Britain's first computer-generated comic. He lectures in computer graphics at London Guildhall University and is also an editor of *Underground*. His forthcoming book *'Invisibles'* furthers the textual and design techniques he has explored in the article here and will be published by Underground in the near future. Contact Graham at PO Box 3285, London, SW2 3NN, UK.

Stephen Metcalf is a designer sadist, exploring the inner edge of delirium and psychosis under the guiding principle of "*murderous on paper, cruel in dreams*", with the aim of proliferating England's moral decline. Contact c/o Postgraduate Pigeonholes, Dept of Cultural Studies, Muirhead Tower, University of Birmingham, Birmingham, B15 2TT, UK.

Marko Lehanka is a German artist who, amongst other things, uses self-written text-generation programmes to mass-produce high velocity soap operas. We are currently unable to retrace him. If anyone can help out with this, please get in touch at the Underground address.

VNS Matrix is a group of four women artists; Josephine Starrs, Julianne Pierce, Francesca da Rimini and Virginia Barratt . They are commited to redefining the role and image of women in art and technology. *"In the world of computer graphics, women are very much present in easily recognisable forms as they are in traditional cinema and advertising: that is, objectified, stereotyped and fetishised. VNS Matrix aim to subvert this traditional image by creating characters and representations of women who are strong, defiant and active."* *All New Gen* also appears as an interactive computer (art) game resident on an Apple computer. You can contact them at; 22 Dunks St, Parkside, South Australia, Australia 5063.

Mark Pawson, International Postal Art Superstar and Cult Stud, founded the Copyright Violation Squad in 1989. It has branches in the UK and USA. He can be contacted at PO Box 664, London, E3 4QR, UK.

Sadie Plant and **Nick Land** teach in the departments of Cultural Studies at Birmingham University and Philosophy at Warwick University, where they can be reached.

Simon Pope: *"It was way back in '55, back when we were young and growin' up in Memphis. We'd stopped by at the five and dime to grab us some corndogs and fries and maybe a few beers. We'd been hanging around for a while, dropping nickels in the jukebox when Curtis shouts 'Hey Elvis, quit messin' around with that burger, boy, and listen to this...' With the beat of them race records pounding away I saw, there and then, Elvis' life flash before my eyes."* Contact: 153 Lake Road West, Roath, Cardiff, CF2 5PJ, Wales.

Richard Wright: after training as a painter, Richard now makes video animations and installations. He also writes widely on technology and culture and is currently Lecturer in Computer Graphics at London Guildhall University. His latest project is a computer animation about Louis XIV and the technology of the imagination. Address: Digital Imaging Group, London Guildhall University, 41 Commercial Road, London, E1 1LA, UK.

Fast Breeder is the topological equivalent of chaos. A chaos engine harnessed to CUT and paste silicon globules of a FREE future into the present. It is a schizo-collective brain whose evil PLAN is to bring the international LOVE octopus of the underground skidding into zero-grav collision with robotic slaves of the evil techno-corporations.

Fast Breeder BBS is dedicated to the transmission of strange signals; bringing artists, activists and others into uncomfortable proximity.
Radical news from Contra Flow, ciba-feminism, other networks, transgressions of intellectual copyright, Quick-Time movies, seizing the media, zines, enthused and engaged theory, demos, virtual performance, PDS, plus - whatever you fancy.
Conferences currently include; Queer, Media, Publications, Class & Culture, Cyberculture, Networks, Oppositional Graphics, Padded Cell, Tech, Fast Forum, with more being added.